AMERICAN
FOOTBALL
LEGENDS

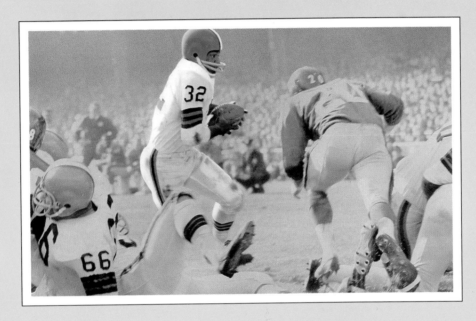

The Greatest Players, Best Games, and Magical Moments—Then and Now

Angus G. Garber III

COLUMBUS
BOOKS

A FRIEDMAN GROUP BOOK

First published in Great Britain in 1988 by Columbus Books Limited
19–23 Ludgate Hill
London, EC4M 7PD, England

British Library Cataloging in Publication Data

Garber, Angus G.
  American football legends.
  1. Football players — Biography
  I. Title
  796.332′092′2   GV939.A1

ISBN 0-86287-924-8

AMERICAN FOOTBALL LEGENDS
was prepared and produced by
Michael Friedman Publishing Group, Inc.
15 West 26th Street
New York, New York 10010

Editor: Bruce Lubin
Art Director: Mary Moriarty
Designer: Rod Gonzalez
Photo Editor: Christopher Bain
Production Manager: Karen L. Greenberg

Typeset by Best-set Typesetter Ltd.
Color separations by South Sea International Press Ltd.
Printed and bound in Hong Kong by Leefung-Asco Printers Ltd.

DEDICATION

For Greg Stone, who taught me the value of words.

ACKNOWLEDGMENTS

Thanks to those whose expertise made this a better product: Vinny DiTrani, the sage of the Bergen Record; Henry Gola, the talented reporter for the New York Post; Kevin Lamb, football expert of the Chicago Sun-Times; Randy Lange, a giant among men; the Elias Sports Bureau; the Pro Football Hall of Fame in Canton, Ohio; the NFL Alumni Association; the public relations men of the NFL; editor Bruce Lubin of the Michael Friedman Publishing Group.

C O N T E N T S

INTRODUCTION
PAGE 8

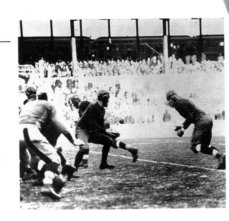
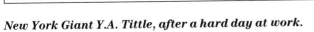

New York Giant Y.A. Tittle, after a hard day at work.

INTRODUCTION

There was a time when professional football didn't captivate the American public, and Super Bowls didn't dominate the sporting scene. Compared to baseball, for example, professional football is a rather recent phenomenon, which underlines its rapid rise to success.

"Back in the early days," says Giants' owner Wellington Mara, "football had no grip at all. It was hardly mentioned in the papers at all. It was regarded around the level of professional wrestling."

Small wonder, for professional football in the early 1900s was a strange business. The collegiate game was revered at the time, but there was something unsavory about professionals and the money they took to play an amateur's game. Jack Cusack, a clerk for the East Ohio Gas Company, and manager of the Canton Bulldogs, helped change all that. In 1913, Cusack hired Jim Thorpe for $250 per game to play for the Bulldogs, and attendance swelled appreciably. Thorpe, who learned the game under Pop Warner at the Carlisle Institute, was the first important professional football player. Many others would follow.

The American Professional Football Association sprung up in 1921 and a year later it became the National Football League. Over the years, there have been many challenges, both in and out of court, but the NFL and its game has always endured. Football is the most demanding of games; it is a stern test of body and soul. Absolute commitment is essential to succeed at it, which might explain the ardor football fans frequently display.

This book celebrates football's greatest legends. Through 1987 there were 133 men enshrined at the Pro Football Hall of Fame in Canton, Ohio — from defensive back Herb Adderley to center/linebacker Alex Wojciechowicz. The greatest of those players are remembered here, along with some of their most glorious games and memorable accomplishments.

This study is in no way definitive — how could it be? Safe to say, however, that these examples represent football's rich pageant. Enjoy them.

The Baltimore Colts and New York Giants battled it out for the 1959 championship.

THE PLAYERS

I n 1987, NFL Films, Inc., undertook a vast project. The company invited experts from around the country to rate the great players in professional football history. The idea was to arrive at some sort of consensus, to name a single team comprised of history's best player at each position.

Predictably, controversy ensued and the project was shelved indefinitely. Apparently, the good folks at NFL Films forgot to include a few notable players on their otherwise copious ballots and several teams became upset. Clearly, while subjectivity can be an intoxicating freedom, it is also potentially dangerous. Stand in a crowded barroom somewhere on Chicago's north side and declare that Walter Payton is the greatest running back of all time. Even if you are not showered by pretzels and beer, your premise could be legitimately challenged — evidence can be presented to support the theory that former Bears Red Grange or Bronko Nagurski or Gale Sayers deserve that title, not to mention Jim Brown or Eric Dickerson.

Such is the difficulty in comparing different eras. Grange, one of the greatest collegiate runners, helped to popularize the sport during the Great Depression. Nagurski helped the Bears to the NFL title after a six-year retirement in 1943. Sayers was one of the game's most beautiful players to watch in the late 1960s. Payton, the running back of the 1980s, has gained more yards than any rusher in history. Grange, Nagurski, and Sayers are all in the Hall of Fame and Payton will assuredly join them there — but who was better? It depends how old the jury is.

Pick a position, flirt with disaster. Was Joe Namath a better quarterback than Otto Graham, or did he just have whiter shoes and better press? Is Charlie Joiner *really* the greatest wide receiver of all time or was Don Hutson the best? Or Don Maynard? Or Raymond Berry? And who was a better center, Jim Ringo or Frank Gatski? Ringo's name is more familiar, but Gatski Played in 11 NFL championship games in 12 years for the Cleveland Browns.

With all of this in mind, consider the following selections. Complaints will be studiously ignored.

See Sammy sling. At a time when running the ball was in fashion, Baugh dared to be different. His passing revolutionized the NFL.

SAMMY BAUGH

When Sammy Baugh broke into the NFL in 1937, running was still the rage, and the mainstay of strategy. When he retired in 1952, the NFL had embraced the air game. Football would never be quite the same and Baugh was the chief reason.

As a boy in Sweetwater, Texas, Baugh used to throw a football through a hanging spare tire — as it swung wildly and when he was on the dead run. Baugh developed into a scrawny 6–foot–2, 180–pound baseball player at Texas Christian University, but coach Dutch Meyer also displayed him as a multi-threat football athlete who dominated the Southwest Conference. When Baugh rolled around the right end there wasn't any way of knowing if he would: 1) throw a forward pass, 2) quick-kick the ball, 3) pitch the ball to a runner behind him or, 4) run it himself. This kind of uncertainty caused opposing defenses enormous problems.

George Marshall, the owner of the Washington franchise, took notice. He had moved his team from Boston after the 1936 season, changed the name from Braves to Redskins, and now he chose Baugh in the first round of the college draft and handed him a $5,000 contract. Coach Ray Flaherty, an old defensive back, wasn't sure about this radical passing attack. "You can't get by up here by just passing like crazy," Flaherty told Baugh. "You're going to have to learn to run." This, to the man who stunned the NFL champion Green Bay Packers 6–0 in the College All-Star Game by completing a touchdown pass to Gaynell Tinsley. Baugh followed through in his debut, completing 11 of 16 passes to beat the New York Giants, 13–3. In the 1937 NFL championship game, Baugh threw three long touchdown passes, for a total of 335 yards. A 35–yard lob to Ed Justice won the game, 28–21. Nonetheless, Baugh remained a single-wing tailback for his first eight years with the Redskins — and he still managed to lead the league in passing three times. In 1944, new coach Dudley DeGroot went to the grudgingly-accepted T-formation that was, in part, influenced by Baugh's success. Baugh made the transition to quarterback, eventually leading NFL passers six times in all. Len Dawson, Roger Staubach, and Ken Anderson remain a distant second in the record books, tied with four passing titles each.

In 1943, Baugh may have become history's most versatile football player to date. That season, Baugh led the NFL in passing, punting, and interceptions. He hauled down 11 interceptions playing as a defensive back and recorded 28 for his career. Oddly, punting was Baugh's strongest suit — he led the league four times in that category. In 1940, Baugh averaged 51.4 yards on 39 kicks, still a record. He averaged 45.1 yards for his career, second on the all-time list to Indianapolis Colts punter Rohn Stark, who hoists half his kicks in the wind-free Hoosier Dome.

Baugh finished his career with 186 passing touchdowns and 21,886 yards completed in the air. In 1945, he completed more than 70 percent of his passes, a record broken by Anderson in 1982. No one will ever approach Baugh's importance to the passing game in professional football. In an era where three yards and a cloud of dust was considered the ultimate mode of travel, Slingin' Sammy Baugh gave the game wings.

Chuck Bednarik (60) watches as New York Giants' receiver Frank Gifford is carried away on a stretcher. The memory of that jarring and controversial hit in 1960 lingers to this day.

CHUCK BEDNARIK

In this age of football specialization, it is sometimes difficult to appreciate players who had the skill and stamina to play both offense and defense well. St. Louis' Roy Green drew a lot of attention in 1981 when he became the first player in over 20 years to catch a touchdown pass and intercept a pass in the same game. His exploits focused new (and merited) attention on Chuck Bednarik, the last of the two-way stars.

Bednarik came from an era when men played both offense and defense as a matter of course. A 6–foot–3, 230–pound center/ linebacker, Bednarik was one of the best at both his positions. He was an All-America at the University of Pennsylvania and was a first-round draft choice of the Philadelphia Eagles in 1949. World War II service had delayed his college career, but the 24–year-

old Bednarik forced the Eagles to move All-Pro center Vic Lindskog elsewhere. Philadelphia soon discovered Bednarik was their best linebacker, too.

Bednarik quickly gained a reputation as football's "Iron Man." He missed the first two regular season games of his rookie year and then sat out only one other game in a distinguished 14–year career. There may never have been a player who served two masters with more skill. Bednarik was a terrific blocker. He was twice named to the Pro Bowl as a center and in 1969 he was named as the NFL's all-time center. Still, it was his play at line-backer that left opponents and spectators wincing.

For Bednarik played the game in an ill humor, much the way Dick Butkus did. It was a toughness developed in the steel towns of Pennsylvania and later honed by his experience as a gunner on a bomber during World War II. "I was born in a situation where you fought for everything you got," Bednarik says today. "I came from the south side of the tracks where you got in a couple of fights every week."

As a linebacker he was considered a reckless, terrifying defensive force. At least former Giant Frank Gifford certainly feels that way. In the eighth game of the 1960 season, Bednarik leveled Gifford in one of football's most controversial tackles. The Eagles were nursing a seven-point lead, but the Giants were driving with two minutes left in the game. Bednarik's hit left Gifford unconscious and his fumble was recovered by Philadelphia. Leaping in the air with ecstasy at the change in possession, Bednarik drew the wrath of the Giants fans. They assumed he was rejoicing at the fate of Gifford, who would retire for a season after Bednarik's jolting tackle.

In the 1960 NFL championship game, Bednarik similarly disposed of Green Bay running back Paul Hornung. Then, as time ran out, Bednarik saved the 17–13 game for Philadelphia. He played 58 minutes in that game and as Jim Taylor headed for the end zone, Bednarik rose to meet him. On the game's last play, Bednarik drove Taylor to the ground, short of a touchdown.

"Even at the age of 62, I don't like to lose," Bednarik now says. "I want to win no matter what I'm doing — even if it's playing golf or acting as a sales representative. I'm a bad loser."

And a winner to the end.

GEORGE BLANDA

He did not have the soft-as-silk moves of Gale Sayers, or the electric presence of Otto Graham. He did not have the athletic gifts of Jim Brown or the killer instinct of Dick Butkus. But George Blanda had staying power: He played in four different decades, appearing in a total of 340 games over 26 seasons — all uncharted territory in the history of the NFL.

Blanda played until the age of 48, and admits that he was ultimately fired from each of the four teams he played for. Still, he scored 2,002 points in the process, a professional football record (placekicker Jan Stenerud stands more than 300 points behind in second place). Blanda holds all or part of 21 championship game and 16 regular season records.

The Chicago Bears chose the 6-foot-2, 215-pound University of Kentucky athlete in the 12th round of the 1949 draft and, after a brief tenure with the Baltimore Colts, Blanda settled in as a back-up quarterback and kicking specialist. For two of his ten years with the Bears, Blanda was the starting quarterback and, in 1953 Blanda led the NFL in attempts and completions. However, Blanda primarily kicked field goals and extra points. When Chicago waived him in 1959, Blanda sat out a year then signed with the Houston Oilers of the American Football League where he enjoyed his first renaissance.

Blanda led the Oilers to their only two AFL titles (in 1960 and 1961) and became one of the young league's most efficient quarterbacks. He led the league in pass completions from 1963–65, a three year reign that remains unequaled today. In 1967, after the Oilers released him, the Oakland Raiders rescued Blanda from another forced retirement.

Then came the 1970 football season. At age 43, Blanda produced a series of startling game results that eventually carried him to the Hall of Fame. On October 25, Blanda relieved Daryle Lamonica at quarterback and threw three touchdown passes and kicked a field goal to break a 7–7 tie and bury Pittsburgh. Blanda's 48–yard field goal with three seconds left carried Oakland to a 17–17 tie with Kansas City a week later. The game against Cleveland the following week became another Blanda showcase: He threw a touchdown pass with 1:34 remaining and then kicked a 52–yard field goal as the clock ran out to beat the Browns 23–20. The incredible performances continued a week later when Blanda's 20–yard scoring pass with 2:28 left beat Denver 24–19. Then, on November 22 against San Diego, Blanda's field goal with seven seconds left lifted the Raiders to a 20–17 triumph.

Blanda finished his career with Oakland in 1975, having thrown 4,007 passes for 26,920 yards and 236 touchdowns. He also kicked 335 field goals and 943 extra points, a testament to Blanda's enduring value to the teams and league for which he played.

Here is George Blanda doing what he did best for 26 seasons. That's Raiders' quarterback Ken Stabler with the best view in the house.

Though people remember him primarily as a placekicker — and a good one at that — Blanda was a gifted quarterback as well, and operated for many years behind center Jim Otto. In 1970, at age 43, (far right) he made headlines with his extraordinary passing and kicking.

TERRY BRADSHAW

Fred Roe

Terry Bradshaw never got much respect. The Pittsburgh Steelers had already won Super Bowls IX and X when they faced the Dallas Cowboys in Super Bowl XIII, and yet the Cowboys' flamboyant linebacker, Hollywood Henderson, wasn't impressed. "Terry Bradshaw," Henderson mused, "couldn't spell cat if you spotted him the 'c' and the 'a'."

Strong stuff. And then Bradshaw went out and completed 17 of 30 passes for a record 318 yards and four touchdowns. The Steelers won, 35–31. "Ask Henderson if he thinks I'm dumb now," Bradshaw said after he was named the game's Most Valuable Player.

After his 14–year career ended in 1983, after the Shreveport, Louisiana native had completed 2,025 passes for 27,989 yards and 212 touchdowns, there wasn't much fanfare. In many circles, Bradshaw isn't considered among the greatest quarterbacks to play the game, which is unfair. Certainly, Bradshaw had talented teammates — Lynn Swann and John Stallworth were marvelous receivers — but Bradshaw took the Steelers to four Super Bowl titles, something no other man accomplished. Twice, he was the game's MVP.

The stigma may have had its origins in Bradshaw's early NFL days. He came from Woodlawn High School, the same school that produced Buffalo quarterback Joe Ferguson, and enrolled at Louisiana Tech. Bradshaw had an incredibly powerful arm and was remarkably accurate, a rarity for such a flamethrower. The Steelers, who had lost 13 of 14 games in 1969, made him their first round draft choice in 1970. For the next five years, Bradshaw spent much of his time bouncing between the field and the bench. He led the league in interceptions his rookie season, making the always rough adjustment to pro defense.

In 1975, Bradshaw watched Joe Gilliam complete 65 percent of his passes including 12 touchdown passes in six exhibition games. By the time the Steelers reached Super Bowl IX, however, Bradshaw was calling the signals. The Steelers beat the Minnesota Vikings 16–6 and Bradshaw completed 9 of 14 passes, including a touchdown (and no interceptions). In Super Bowl X, Bradshaw was on the delivery end of four magnificent catches by Swann totaling 161 yards — including a spectacular 64–yard touchdown. Bradshaw went 9–for–19 with two touchdowns and, again, no interceptions. Quiet, effective work.

A year after the Steelers defeated the Cowboys in Super Bowl XIII, Bradshaw displayed courage through adversity. At the Rose Bowl in Pasadena, California, he had a dismal first half of Super Bowl XIV, suffering three interceptions at the hands of the Los Angeles Rams. Three minutes into the second half, Bradshaw erased a 13–10 deficit with a 47–yard scoring play to Swann. With the Rams leading 19–17 early in the fourth quarter, Bradshaw delivered victory to the Steelers one more time. On third-and–8 at his own 27–yard line, Bradshaw heaved the ball just over the fingertips of cornerback Rod Perry into the hands of Stallworth, who raced 73 yards with the winning touchdown. The Steelers had tried the play eight times in practices leading up to the game and had never been successful. "This time it went," Bradshaw said. "I just unloaded." Hardly a cerebral explanation, but effective nonetheless. Sort of like Terry Bradshaw.

Although in many circles Terry Bradshaw was not considered a great quarterback, he did manage to take the Pittsburgh Steelers to four Super Bowl titles. No one else has ever done that.

Fred Roe

Here is the essence of Jim Brown: He averaged 5.2 yards every time he carried the ball, a mark that is far and away football's best.

JIM BROWN

Jim Brown was arguably the greatest running back in the history of the NFL.

He played only nine seasons — a brief term, compared to some of football history's more talented rushers — but each was spectacular — and totally dominant. Brown was named to the Pro Bowl each of his nine years, a record that underscores his consistent brilliance. Eight of those years, Brown led the NFL in rushing. The nearest competitors in that category, O.J. Simpson and Steve Van Buren, won four titles each. How ethereal was Brown? He holds the NFL record for leading the league in rushing five consecutive years — and he is tied with Van Buren and Earl Campbell for second place, with a three year run at the top.

Brown was a first round draft choice of the Cleveland Browns in 1957 after earning All-America status the year before at Syracuse, although the Browns would have taken quarterback Len Dawson of Purdue if the Steelers hadn't drafted him one spot earlier. In a debut that has never been matched, Brown ran away with the league's Rookie of the Year honors and was also named Player of the Year. On November 24, Brown scorched the Los Angeles Rams for 237 yards, a team record only he would eventually match.

In 1958, Brown was named the NFL's Most Valuable Player after rushing for 1,527 yards. The numbers piled up in quick succession.

In 1963, his best season, Brown rushed 291 times for 1,863 yards, an average of 6.4 yards per carry. Brown had that rare combination of size and speed. At 6–foot–2 and 228 pounds, Brown was big enough to level linebackers yet quick enough to outrun defensive backs. His acceleration at the line of scrimmage was phenomenal; his consistency no less impressive. He never missed a game during his career and managed to carry the ball at least 200 times each season. Brown was also a gifted pass receiver, grabbing 262 career catches, worth 2,499 yards.

After the 1965 season, Brown shocked the football world by walking away from the game. He had enjoyed the second best year of his career (1,544 yards), but at the age of 29, Brown decided to leave on top. He pursued a new career in Hollywood and eventually landed a prominent role in *The Dirty Dozen*. Acting, however, didn't come as easily to Brown as running with the football. How could it?

In 1984, his tenth season, Chicago's Walter Payton broke Brown's all-time rushing record of 12,321 yards. Payton later tied Brown's touchdown standard of 106 in the 1986, but in one vital statistic he is not yet Brown's equal. Through 12 seasons Payton has averaged 4.4 yards per carry. Brown averaged 5.2 yards each time he ran with the ball — a record that may never be equaled.

Jim Brown was always intent on crossing the goal line. Although he played for only nine seasons, the records he set have taken much longer to break. If, for a few years, he had resisted the temptation to make movies, Jim Brown's numbers might have been unassailable.

Fred Roe

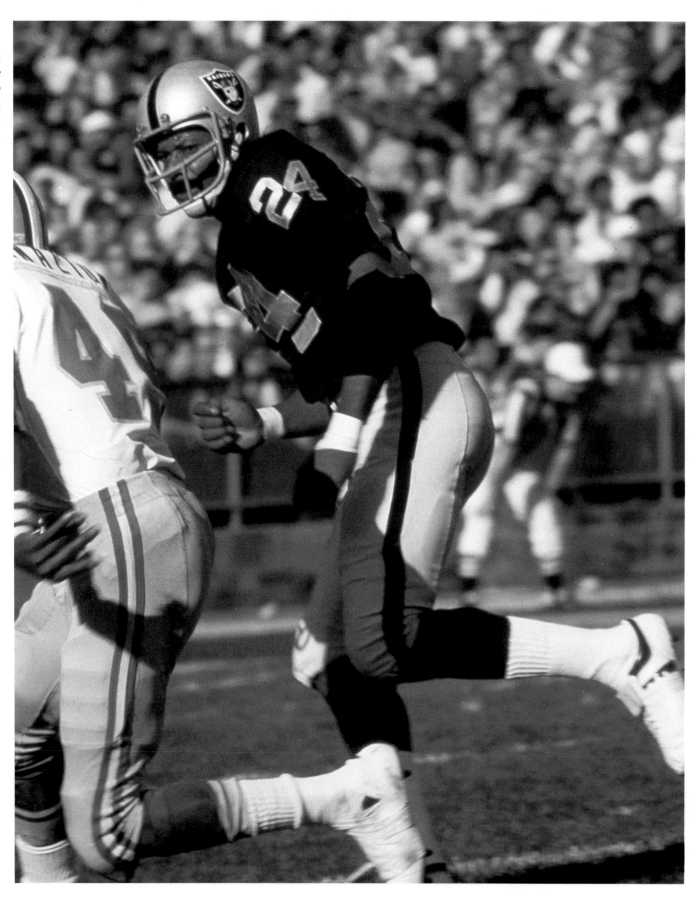

Willie Brown developed a technique for covering receivers that is considered textbook today.

WILLIE BROWN

Like many great innovations, Willie Brown's gift to football was discovered quite by accident.

He had been a tight end at Grambling, and an anonymous one at that. At 6–foot–1, 217 pounds, Brown was used primarily as a blocker. Though his collegiate performance didn't inspire any professional football team to draft him, Brown signed with the AFL's Houston Oilers as a free agent in 1963. Coach Frank "Pop" Ivy took one look at Brown and decided he was a defensive back.

"I was kind of surprised," says Brown, who became the Raiders' defensive backs coach in 1979, "So I said, 'Why not?'"

After a few weeks, an idea came to Brown as he was practicing his backpedaling steps. Why, he wondered, did defensive backs set up five to eight yards off the line of scrimmage?

"I didn't make any sense to me," Brown says. "I mean, if I was on the line of scrimmage, right in a guy's face, I was big enough so I could get my hands on him and fast enough so no one could outrun me."

The coaching staff thought Brown was crazy. After another week of displaying this bizarre new technique Brown was asked to leave. He surfaced with the Denver Broncos and managed to stick with the team as an avant-garde cornerback. Soon Brown and the Broncos were getting calls from around the league. They wanted to know how Brown did it. Gradually, Brown's bump-and-run technique became an accepted form of defense — the quickest way to shut down a potent wide receiver at the line of scrimmage.

Sixteen years after the Oilers sent him packing, Brown was recognized as one of the greatest cornerbacks ever to play the game, perhaps the best of all time. Brown played his last 12 seasons with the Oakland Raiders and finished with 54 career interceptions. Other defensive backs (Paul Krause had 81 career thefts and Emlen Tunnell finished with 79) pulled down more interceptions, but Brown didn't have their opportunities — for much of his career, quarterbacks avoided throwing at his zone. In the 14 game season of 1971, for instance, only ten opponents' passes were completed in Brown's sector. An incredible, telling statistic.

Not that Brown didn't set a few records of his own. He intercepted at least one pass in each of his 16 seasons, a feat unequaled by any other defensive back. His footwork and work habits were the reason for that marvelous consistency. Though his speed diminished slightly over the years, Brown always seemed to find a way to get back into position.

On November 15, 1964, Brown intercepted four passes in a single game, a record which stands to this day. In Super Bowl X, Brown intercepted a Minnesota pass and returned it 75 yards for a touchdown and another piece of history.

Since 1979, Brown has been teaching the Raiders' rookie defensive backs the bump-and-run technique he invented and ultimately perfected. He has a lot of patience. "You never know when you're going to learn something," Brown says. "Some rookie might have a crazy idea that actually works."

27

Today, Dick Butkus is almost lovable in his pitches for national products. Do not be fooled; he was one of the meanest players in NFL history.

DICK BUTKUS

Fred Roe

The game was already hopelessly out of hand — the Detroit Lions led the Chicago Bears 40–7 with only 30 seconds on the clock. Chicago linebacker Dick Butkus, limping on a ravaged right knee and playing in what would be the second-to-last game of his brilliant nine year career, inexplicably called a time out.

Now, his teammates liked to win as much as anyone, but this was a little ridiculous. The Lions, who assumed the Bears would let the clock run out, ran another play and Butkus called another timeout. Doug Buffone, the outside linebacker who played alongside Butkus for eight seasons, was mystified.

"I couldn't figure it out," Buffone says today, "it was over and he's playing like a madman. Then it dawned on me. He had been having this war with their center, a guy named Ed Flanagan. I watched him after the second time out and, sure enough, he took a run at him and really drilled him. Then, he called our last timeout and did it again.

"That is how I remember Dick Butkus. His intensity was incredible. If I hit a guy, there was a 99 percent chance he'd get up. If Dick hit a guy, there was a good chance he wouldn't get up."

To the end, Butkus was a fierce competitor. That fire, and inability to admit defeat, made him one of the game's greatest linebackers. Some people say he was just plain nasty.

Butkus' uneven temperament had first become obvious when he was a 6–foot–3, 245–pound, two time All-America linebacker at the University of Illinois. The Bears won a bidding war with the Denver Broncos and watched with delight as the third place finisher in the Heisman Trophy race mauled the Cleveland Browns with 15 total tackles and a blocked field goal during an exhibition game. It was clear that Butkus would be asked to fill the shoes of Bill George, the middle linebacker of George Halas' Monsters of the Midway. In the season opener against San Francisco, Butkus made 11 unassisted tackles, laying aside all doubts.

When Butkus tackled, he didn't merely take the man down — he punished him. Intimidation was his calling card; no other player in football history consistently hit with such severity. Butkus wasn't blessed with great speed, but his unnatural anticipation always delivered him to the ball on time.

Butkus played in eight consecutive Pro Bowls and finished his career with 22 career interceptions and 25 fumble recoveries. One can only guess how many fumbles his bone rattling hits caused — the NFL doesn't keep such records.

The last two years of Butkus' abbreviated career were hindered by the pain in his right knee. "I used to be in the hole before it opened up," Butkus told teammates, "now, I'm one step behind."

Yet in his prime, Butkus was always a step ahead.

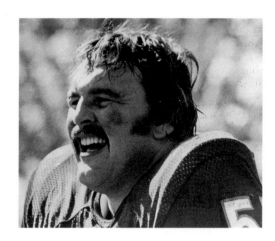

(below) Here is classic Butkus: Green Bay's Dave Hampton wants to go forward, but Chicago's irresistible middle man has other ideas. Many of the NFL's best running backs went backwards when Butkus tackled them.

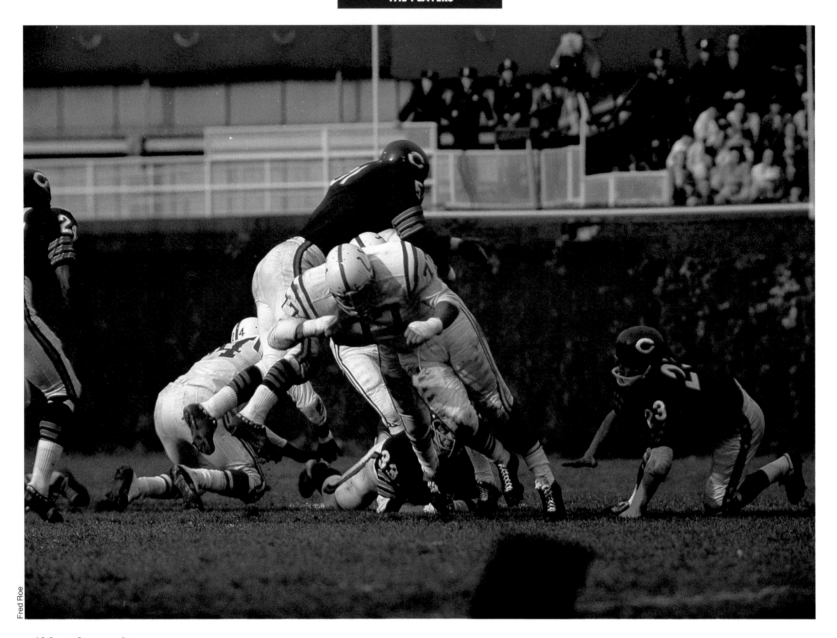

Fred Roe

Although opposing offensive linemen rarely got a lift from him, Butkus brought a new level of play to the game. Today, the Butkus award is given each season to the nation's best collegiate linebacker.

The face of a Bear: Mike Ditka's snarling passion is what distinguished him as a player and a coach.

MIKE DITKA

The fourth game of the 1983 season had just ended and the Chicago Bears had just been handed their third loss, the second in overtime. Furious, Mike Ditka put his fist through a metal locker and calmly called for the team doctor. Ditka — the Bears coach — had broken his hand.

As a player, it was this kind of passion that made Ditka an on-field alter-ego of feisty George Halas, the Bears' founder and guiding force. Ditka, at 6–foot–3, 225 pounds, was the prototypical tight end, and he played the game like a linebacker on a bad Monday morning after a worse Sunday night.

Born in Carnegie, Pennsylvania, Ditka carried a powerful work ethic to the University of Pittsburgh, where he played end and middle linebacker on defense, and blocking end on offense. And when those two units were on the sidelines, Ditka was a punter as well. Recognizing his rarely used pass–receiving talents, the Bears drafted the All-America in the first round of the 1961 draft. To that point, tight ends were employed almost exclusively as blockers. Then Halas unleashed Ditka on an unsuspecting NFL.

As a rookie, he caught 56 passes for 1,076 yards and 12 touchdowns. For each of the next three years, Ditka was voted to the Pro Bowl. He caught 58 passes in 1962, another 59 in the championship year of 1963, and in 1964, Ditka reeled in 75 receptions — a league record for tight ends that stood until San Diego's Kellen Winslow broke it in 1980. All the while, Ditka was a devastating blocker.

In 1967, Chicago reluctantly traded Ditka to Philadelphia in exchange for quarterback Jack Concannon. The Eagles used Ditka sparingly and two years later sent him to Dallas, where he played in two Super Bowl games. In Super Bowl VI, his last game as a player, Ditka scored the last touchdown on a seven-yard pass from Roger Staubach. Ditka's career numbers: 427 catches, 5,812 yards, 43 touchdowns.

Dallas coach Tom Landry asked Ditka to remain with the team as the tight end and special teams coach. In the nine years Ditka was an assistant, the Cowboys made the playoffs eight times and reached the Super Bowl three times. Before Ditka left to coach Chicago, he developed three Pro Bowl receivers in Dallas : Billy Joe Dupree, Drew Pearson, and Tony Hill.

Finally, in 1982, Halas called Ditka home again. The Bears suffered a 3–6 record in Ditka's strike-shortened first season, and followed with an 8–8 record which included that broken hand. Two years later, the Bears finally displayed Ditka's wicked spirit and smashed through the regular season to a 15–1 record. After two playoff shutouts, the Bears crushed the New England Patriots, 46–10, in Super Bowl XX. With the happy conclusion of the 20th Super Bowl, Ditka had played or coached in six of them.

Fred Roe

34

FORREST GREGG

Forrest Gregg had a nose for football — a marvelous feel for the game. In many ways, Gregg was the prototypical football player. Vince Lombardi, for one, thought so.

Consider the great players from coach Vince Lombardi's glory days with the Green Bay Packers: Bart Starr, Ray Nitschke, Herb Adderley, Willie Davis, Paul Hornung, Jim Ringo, Jim Taylor. All of them, including Lombardi himself, are enshrined in Pro Football's Hall of Fame in Canton, Ohio. Yet there was one player Lombardi believed was better than all of them. "Forrest Gregg," Lombardi once said, "is the finest player I ever coached."

Go ahead and argue with that. Gregg, at 6–foot–4, 250 pounds, was one of football's great offensive linemen and he stood out even among the giants of the game. Together with Ringo, a center, and guard Jerry Kramer, Gregg helped comprise what most experts view as the greatest offensive line of all time. In 15 years as a professional, Gregg played on six NFL championship teams. He was a winner in the purest sense of the word.

Gregg was born in Birthright, Texas in 1933 and attended Southern Methodist University, where he was an All-Southwest Conference two-way tackle. The Packers chose him in the second round of the 1956 draft, but a year later Gregg served a 21-month hitch in the military. Though he originally had designs on a defensive career, Gregg was persuaded his future lay on offense as a tackle and, later, a guard.

The hallmark of great offensive linemen is their balance and intelligence, and Gregg was exceptional in both respects. He could steer a charging defensive lineman just about anywhere he

wanted and was rarely beaten when he was pass-blocking. He was also an aggressive run-blocker. Starr's lifetime statistics reflect the protection he got and both Hornung and Taylor owe a measure of their fame to Gregg, who often toiled anonymously.

He played in 188 consecutive games, with the only near miss coming in 1965 when a severely bruised knee prevented Gregg from starting. He went in to block for an extra point, however, and the streak stayed alive. Several times Gregg tried to retire and on every occasion coaches who needed him in the lineup prevailed. In 1963, Gregg actually accepted an assistant coaching job at the University of Tennessee but Lombardi talked him out of it. Then in 1969 and 1970, Gregg began each year as an assistant to Phil Bengston, only to finish the season in uniform.

When Gregg stepped aside a fourth time Dallas coach Tom Landry asked him to play one final season. Four years after the Packers had won back-to-back Super Bowls, Gregg helped carry the Cowboys to their first NFL championship.

In 1982, Gregg was back at Super Bowl XVI in a new role, as the coach of the Cincinnati Bengals. He had led the Bengals to the league's best record over the 1981 and 1982 seasons, but decided to return as Green Bay's head coach in 1983. The Packers, who had fallen into a decline after Lombardi left in 1967, were looking for some respect. With Lombardi gone, his finest player was the next best thing.

DON HUTSON

In the subjective business of football greatness, arguments are unavoidable in most cases. Not so with Green Bay Packer Don Hutson.

Hutson is acknowledged by most observers as the greatest end in the history of professional football and he profoundly changed the game's direction. Along with quarterback Sammy Baugh, Hutson in his brilliant career (1935–1945) forced the transition from run-dominated strategy to the high-flying passing game of modern football.

His records have worn well with time. For eight seasons, Hutson led the NFL in touchdowns scored — running back Jim Brown and receiver Lance Alworth are a distant second, with three touchdown titles each. Hutson led the league's receivers in receptions eight different times, and led in total yardage seven times, records which are as unassailable as any in history. Hutson finished his career with 488 catches, 7,981 yards and 100 touchdowns — all achieved at a time when passing was considered a desperation measure.

"We didn't throw the ball much in those days," Hutson remembers. "At Alabama, we passed 12, maybe 15 times a game, which was a lot by those standards. Now, they fling it every chance they get."

Blame Hutson. At 6–foot–1, 180 pounds, he had the perfect sprinter's body. When Jesse Owens set a world record of 9.4 seconds in the 100–yard dash in 1936, Hutson was recording consistent clockings of 9.7. And yet there was more to him than speed.

"You can be as fast as the wind," Hutson says, "but it doesn't mean anything if you can't catch the ball. That's what I prided myself on."

Hutson had sure hands and a sensational leaping ability, but more importantly, a remarkable mind that always managed to help him get into position for the important catch. Indeed, Hutson was the first receiver to run conventional pass patterns. It began at Alabama when quarterback Dixie Howell discovered he had an advantage over opposing defensive backs — he knew where Hutson was going. By deciding on prearranged routes, Howell could throw just as Hutson was making his move.

The Packers and the Brooklyn Dodgers had seen Hutson in the 1935 Rose Bowl and tendered contract offers. Hutson signed them both, but the Packers were awarded his rights when the league determined their contract had been in the mail first — by 17 minutes.

Arnie Herber and Hutson combined for an 83–yard touchdown in Hutson's professional debut, a 7–0 victory over Chicago. Defenses quickly took notice, often assigning two or three players to cover Hutson. Usually, he found a way to get loose. In one game against the Cleveland Rams, Hutson was running from his left end position at full-speed, diagonally toward the right goal post. Hutson reached the goal post and hooked the upright with his left arm, letting his momentum spin him around the other way. Just as he looked down field, Cecil Isbell's pass landed in Hutson's right hand for a touchdown.

Hutson's receiving talents overshadowed his ability as a defensive back. As was the practice of the times, Hutson played all 60 minutes. In his last four seasons, he intercepted a total of 23 passes. In his later seasons, Hutson was a placekicker who added nearly 200 points to Packers' totals.

Hutson, it seemed, was always ahead of his time. In 1942, he caught 74 passes, a staggering total even by today's standards, but incomprehensible at the time. Consider: 24 receptions took second place that season. When he retired, Hutson had caught nearly 300 career passes more than Jim Benton, the runner-up at the time.

Deacon Jones practically invented the term quarterback sack and mastered it, too, as San Francisco quarterback John Brodie (right) knows. A rare combination of size and speed made Jones so dangerous, he changed forever the way personnel men looked at defensive ends.

DAVID "DEACON" JONES

You take greatness where you can find it, and in 1961 the Los Angeles Rams found an obscure defensive end from Mississippi Vocational in the 14th round of the college draft. His name was David Jones — he hadn't invented the name "Deacon" yet, or a whole lot of other things, for that matter.

When he retired after the 1974 season, Jones had created a standard against which all future defensive linemen would be measured. He was the first of the swift, hulking quarterback stalkers. The acceleration of the passing game caught defenses by surprise in the 1950s, but Jones' play was a bold, flamboyant counter stroke. If teams insisted on traveling by air, they were going to have to pay the fare.

That resulted in more than a few mangled signal-callers. The Rams' "Fearsome Foursome" that featured Jones, Merlin Olsen, Roosevelt Grier, and Lamar Lundy was one of football's greatest defensive lines. And Jones, despite Olsen's record of 14 Pro Bowl appearances, was the leading light. He stood over 6–foot–4 and weighed 272 pounds and the power he generated was enormous. It was Jones who coined the term "sacks" for those instances when quarterbacks were tackled behind the line of scrimmage. Lawrence Taylor notwithstanding, Jones mastered the sack. Though the NFL didn't start keeping sack totals until 1972, Rams statistics give some indication of Jones' dominance. In 1967, Los Angeles quarterbacks were trapped 25 times, while Jones decked opposing quarterbacks 26 times alone.

Born in Eatonville, Florida in 1938, Jones played football at both South Carolina State and Mississippi Vocational. Rams' scouts, watching game films of a running back prospect, couldn't believe the huge defender who seemed to outrun their man on nearly every play. Jones made an instant impression in training camp and over the years refined his game to a science. He had it all: Great strength, raw speed, moves. In addition to his never–before–seen acceleration off the line, Jones invented a variety of techniques that helped him slip past blockers. His helmet slap — a disorienting blow that is technically illegal but rarely called as a foul — is now an accepted weapon in every defensive end's arsenal.

Unlike many football innovators, Jones was recognized by his peers. He was voted to eight Pro Bowls and was named the NFL's Defensive Player of the Year in 1967. That was the season the 11–1–2 Rams won their first conference title in 13 years. In 1968, the Rams defense set a 14–game NFL record for fewest yards allowed.

After 11 years with the Rams, Jones played two seasons with San Diego and then was reunited with coach George Allen for a final campaign in Washington. Allen loved the way Jones approached the game, calling him the best practice player he ever saw. Even when there was nothing on the line, Jones was inventing situations that made him the best.

Bob Lilly (here on the prowl against the St. Louis Cardinals) was arguably the best trade the Dallas Cowboys ever made. The local boy made good immediately and eventually maximized his unusual ability by moving from end to tackle.

BOB LILLY

Bob Lilly was always first in the hearts of the Dallas Cowboys' fans — from day one of the franchise.

In 1961, he was the new franchise's first draft choice. A year later, Lilly was the Cowboys' first player selected to the Pro Bowl. In 1964, he was their first all-league performer; in 1972 Lilly helped Dallas win its first Super Bowl. And people wonder why he's called "Mr. Cowboy."

At 6–foot–5, 260 pounds, Lilly was a nearly perfect defensive tackle. He had quickness to go with that size and a football intellect that was unrivaled. For 14 seasons, Lilly pressured opposing defenses and 11 different times he was named to the Pro Bowl. Incredibly, Lilly might have made an even bigger impact on the game if he had been left to develop as a defensive end.

The Cowboys were awarded a NFL franchise in 1960 and a year later the organization contemplated its first college draft. They promptly traded their first pick, the second overall, to the Washington Redskins for quarterback Eddie LeBaron. The Cowboys would build the early offense around LeBaron and he would hold the fort until Don Meredith arrived in 1963. What of the defense? Dallas traded tackle Paul Dickson and its 1962 first round pick to Cleveland for the right to draft Lilly.

He had been performing under the Cowboys' noses at nearby Texas Christian University, where twice Lilly was named to the All-Southwest Conference team. Dallas saw him as a defensive end. Their vision was hardly faulty; Lilly was voted the NFL's Rookie of the Year and made his first visit to the Pro Bowl a year later. As gifted as his performances were, the Cowboys wondered if a move to the inside might better take advantage of Lilly's great strength. Most of history's outstanding pass rushers are ends because they can take wide, looping routes to the quarterback. Tackles have to power through the mess along the line of scrimmage, often fending off three different blockers. Lilly was an exception to the rule. Freed from the constraints of containing the outside lane, Lilly was left with only the quarterback in his sights. The results were devastating. Lilly anchored the unit that would become known as Dallas' "Doomsday Defense." The cast of characters around him changed often, but Lilly remained steadfast, playing in 292 games, including 196 consecutive regular season contests — he missed only one game over those 14 years.

With miserable, average, or great teams, Lilly's level of play was consistently excellent. Lilly retired in 1974 and six years later recorded another Dallas first: He became the first Dallas player elected to the Football Hall of Fame.

GINO MARCHETTI

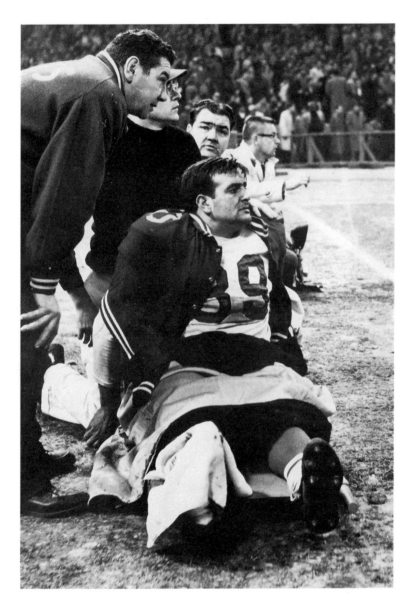

How badly did Gino Marchetti want to play football? After breaking his leg during a 1958 game, he watched the rest of the contest from the sidelines.

From the age of 18, when he fought for the U.S. Army in the Battle of the Bulge, Gino Marchetti had a razor sharp competitive edge. In the combative trenches of the NFL, there was never a more tenacious player. During the NFL's 50th anniversary celebration in 1969, Marchetti was acclaimed as the greatest defensive end in professional football history.

In 14 seasons, Marchetti played in 10 Pro Bowls — it might have been a record of 11 consecutive appearances if not for teammate "Big Daddy" Lipscomb. Marchetti had just made a critical stop on the New York Giants' Frank Gifford in the celebrated 1958 NFL championship game, when Lipscomb, all 300 pounds of him, arrived after the fact. Marchetti's ankle was broken and even though the Colts would win the game in overtime, 23–17, he wasn't able to play in the Pro Bowl game a week later.

After graduation from Antioch High School in California, Marchetti enrolled at the University of San Francisco, where one of his teammates was halfback Ollie Matson, who would later join him in the Pro Football Hall of Fame. Marchetti, a 6–foot–4, 245–pound tackle, played in the East-West and College All-Star games of 1951 and was drafted by the New York Yanks. The troubled franchise became the Dallas Texans for a year before moving to Baltimore in 1953.

Marchetti's size prompted the Colts to try him as an offensive tackle, but soon his defensive talent emerged. Marchetti was a terrific pass rusher. He moved well for a big man and had an overriding desire to reach the quarterback. Opponents often tried to stop him with double and triple teams, though with little success. Marchetti's pass-rushing technique wasn't always of the textbook variety, but he did his job with brutal effectiveness, often adding the insult of an elbow to a fallen passer. Marchetti was also outstanding against the run.

In 1955, Marchetti was voted by his peers to the Pro Bowl for the first time. The Colts teamed Marchetti with defensive tackle Art Donovan, another future Hall of Famer, and soon opponents were having difficulty scoring. Baltimore won back-to-back NFL championships in 1958 and 1959.

By 1963, Marchetti was a playing assistant coach. He announced his retirement after the season, but reconsidered and played in 1964. Though Marchetti retired again after the 1964 season, the Colts asked him to play once more for a six game stretch when they were decimated by injuries. Marchetti heeded the call — yet another example of his indomitable spirit.

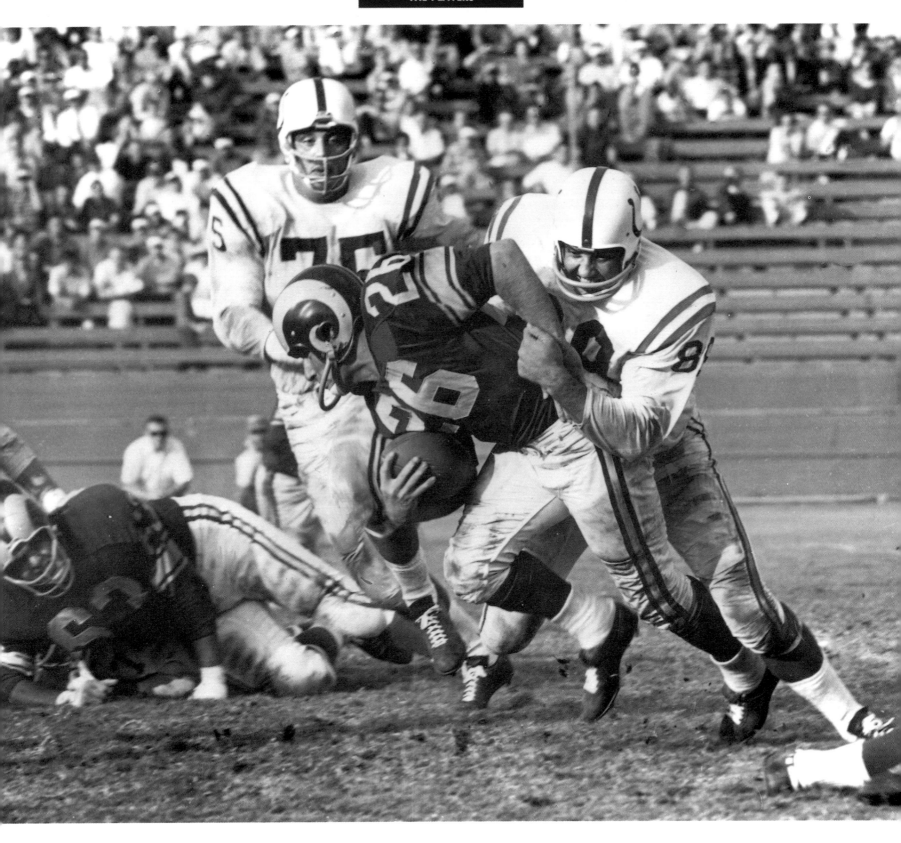

At 6-1, 179 pounds, Don Maynard was not particularly big, nor was he exceptionally fast. All he did was catch the ball — 633 times.

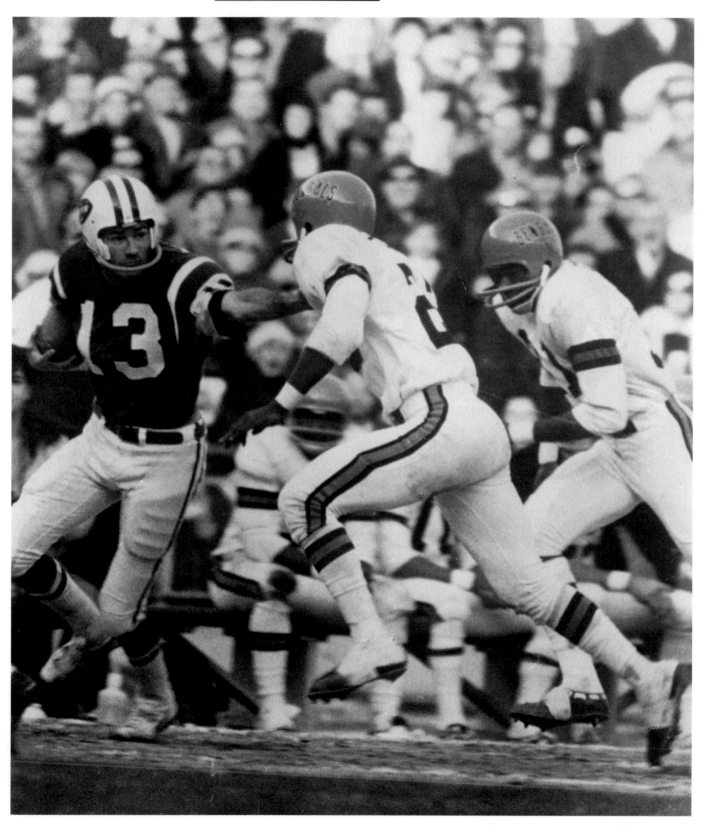

DON MAYNARD

Although he retired in 1973 as the NFL's all-time leading receiver in pass receptions (633) and total yards (11,834), it took Don Maynard nine tries to get elected to Pro Football's Hall of Fame.

This sort of treatment was nothing new for Maynard, who suffered in the shadow of quarterback Joe Namath for 13 years with the New York Jets. Named only once to a major wire service all-AFL team, Maynard was nonetheless chosen as a member of the all-time AFL team when the league closed its doors in 1969. Such was the nature of Maynard's often anonymous career.

Spectacular — in the manner of Paul Warfield, Elroy "Crazy-legs" Hirsch, or Lenny Moore — Maynard was not. He never led his league in receiving, but he is one of only five players to catch more than 50 passes and gain more than 1,000 yards in five different seasons. Maynard also recorded 50 different 100–yard games, a record that still stands.

Part of it was his lean 6–foot–1, 179–pound frame: Maynard did not seem equipped to deal with the rigors of a game based on aggressive behavior. Another factor was Maynard's entrance into professional football, which was hardly auspicious. He was a free Texas spirit, exhibiting a cavalier attitude that probably was shaped by attending eight different grade schools and five high schools. He played college ball at Rice and Texas Western before the New York Giants drafted him for the 1958 season. Maynard mishandled a few punts and the Giants quickly decided they didn't need an ambling cowboy with sideburns, dungarees, and boots — especially one with bad hands. Maynard sought refuge in Canada, where he played one season for the Winnipeg Blue Bombers.

In 1960 a new sports enterprise was born and Maynard became the first player to sign with the New York Titans of the new American Football League. Coach Sammy Baugh, an innovator of the passing game, quickly put Maynard and quarterback Al Dorow to work. Maynard caught 72 passes in his AFL rookie season. Coach Weeb Ewbank arrived in 1963 and Namath joined the team now called the Jets two years later. Maynard, they realized, could be the focal part of the offense.

"He'll kill you one-on-one," said defensive backfield coach Walt Michaels, who would later become the Jets' head coach. "The biggest thing that makes him dangerous is his speed and his change of pace. It's no secret. When many guys come downfield fast, they are going all out, but their all-out speed is about three-quarter speed compared to Maynard."

Maynard and Namath connected on a record nine passes for 128 yards in the 1967 AFL All-Star game and a year later against Miami

Fred Roe

he caught seven passes for 160 yards, which put him in first place for total career receiving yards gained.

Yet even in Super Bowl III later that season, Maynard was passed over, so to speak. Though he entered the game with a leg injury, Namath immediately tested the Baltimore defense with a long pass to Maynard. The ball was slightly overthrown, but the Colts understood immediately that Maynard was a deep threat. They altered their coverage accordingly and Namath was able to reach George Sauer for eight passes and 133 yards. After the Jets' 16–7 upset, the media descended on Namath and Sauer, leaving Maynard alone with his thoughts.

He isn't alone any more. In 1987, Maynard was enshrined in the Hall of Fame.

BRONKO NAGURSKI

He was born in Rainy River, Ontario, Canada, and eventually moved across the border to International Falls, Minnesota. That Bronko Nagurski chose to live in the harsh climate of the northernmost point in the continental United States was somehow appropriate — the fullback for the Chicago Bears was one of the toughest, strongest, hardiest players the game has ever seen. Certainly Nagurski, who gained 4,031 yards in nine seasons, was football's most punishing runner.

Even a grade school teacher recognized his potential for mayhem, translating Nagurski's Ukrainian given name of Bronislau into Bronko. At the University of Minnesota, Nagurski was as good as his name, earning All-America status as a bruising fullback and a defensive tackle as well. During one game his junior year, Nagurski broke three ribs. He played the next week at tackle.

In Chicago, Bears' owner George Halas followed Nagurski's progress with interest. He acquired the 6–foot–2, 225–pounder's services in 1930 and two years later, the Bears had advanced to the National Football League championship game. It was a trend-setting contest on several levels.

The Bears were to meet the Portsmouth Spartans (later the Detroit Lions) at Chicago's Wrigley Field, but snow and minus–30 degree temperatures forced the game inside to Chicago Stadium. It was the first championship game played under a roof. (Forty-six years later, a football playoff final would return indoors with Super Bowl XII, played at the Louisiana Superdome in New Orleans.) The Stadium's field was only 80 yards long and hash marks were employed for the first time to help keep players clear of the nearby concrete stands. The two teams struggled through three scoreless periods before a bit of Nagurski ingenuity won the game. Chicago had reached the Portsmouth 2–yard line when Nagurski took a handoff and appeared headed for the end zone. Suddenly, he stopped short and lofted a short pass to teammate Red Grange. The Spartans protested the play, claiming that Nagurski was not the prescribed five yards behind the line of scrimmage when he released the ball. The play stood, however, and the Bears eventually won 9–0. During the offseason, Halas would lobby to change the rule and, ultimately, the league allowed pass attempts from anywhere behind the line of scrimmage.

Nagurski's ingenuity was called upon again when Chicago defeated the New York Giants in the 1933 championship game, thanks to his two surprise touchdown passes from the fullback position. In 1934, Nagurski gained a career high 586 yards, and his vicious blocks allowed teammate Beattie Feathers to become the NFL's first 1,000–yard rusher. Though Nagurski retired after the 1937 season, he returned six years later when World War II ravaged the Chicago roster. Nagurski started at tackle but found himself in the backfield as the Bears swept to the 1943 championship. Nagurski scored Chicago's first touchdown in a 41–21 victory over Washington, proving at the age of 35 he was still perhaps football's toughest competitor.

Bronko Nagurski was an aggressive player, even in the rough-and-tumble early days of the NFL. Some of those who tried to tackle him thought Nagurski's real forte might have been defense.

Big Jim Parker worked hard at protecting Baltimore Colts' quarterback Johnny Unitas. The offensive lineman was one of the reasons the Colts were at the top of their game in the 1950s.

JIM PARKER

He was a pioneer, an imposing combination of size, speed, and talent who defined the position of offensive lineman for a modern generation. In 1973, Jim Parker was enshrined in the Pro Football Hall of Fame, the first player elected exclusively as an offensive lineman. Those who don't carry, throw, or catch the football are often anonymous, but Parker's 11–year career with the Baltimore Colts is hard to overlook.

At 6–foot–3, 273 pounds, Parker was one of the giants of his day. At the same time, he had the critical tools necessary to protect the quarterback as the passing game grew in importance: agile feet, quick hands, and finesse rare for a man so large.

At Scott High School in Toledo, Ohio, it seemed improbable. Though Parker was only a fourth team All-State selection his senior year, Ohio State coach Woody Hayes saw possibilities and recruited him for the Buckeyes in 1953. Impressed with Parker's versatility, Hayes used him as a guard on offense and a linebacker on defense. During Parker's sophomore year, Ohio State won the Rose Bowl and the national championship. He was an All-America his last two seasons and won the Outland Trophy in 1956 as the nation's outstanding collegiate lineman. Thirteen years later, Parker would be named to the modern all-time All-America college football team.

Parker's greatest triumphs came as a guard, but Hayes remained convinced his future was on defense, and told the Colts that when they chose Parker in the first round of the 1957 draft. Baltimore, however, had different ideas. They had drafted Southern Methodist end Raymond Berry in 1954, then added Penn State flanker Lenny Moore, and Johnny Unitas, (then a nondescript free agent quarterback from Louisville), in 1956. Eventually, Berry, Moore, and Unitas would all join Parker — the prime protector of their passing art — in the Hall of Fame.

Hayes always said, "Three things can happen when you throw the ball — and two of them are bad." Thus, Parker never learned much pass-blocking technique at run-oriented Ohio State. His education, however, came in a hurry:The Colts threw 47 passes in Baltimore's first exhibition game. Unitas would pass 301 times in Parker's rookie season and the Colts had their first winning record in nine years of existence. Baltimore finished with matching 9–3 records in 1958 and 1959 and both times went on to defeat the New York. Giants in memorable NFL championship games.

In 1962, the Colts moved Parker from tackle to left guard. The positions are side by side, but the responsibilities are quite different. As a guard, Parker would have to block larger defensive tackles, instead of the more mobile defensive ends. The transition was a smooth one and Parker, who had been named to the Pro Bowl all four years at tackle, enjoyed the honor four more seasons as a guard. In 1966, Baltimore switched him back to tackle, where a leg injury ended his ground-breaking career in 1967.

Parker was not only the first great offensive lineman: He might have been the best.

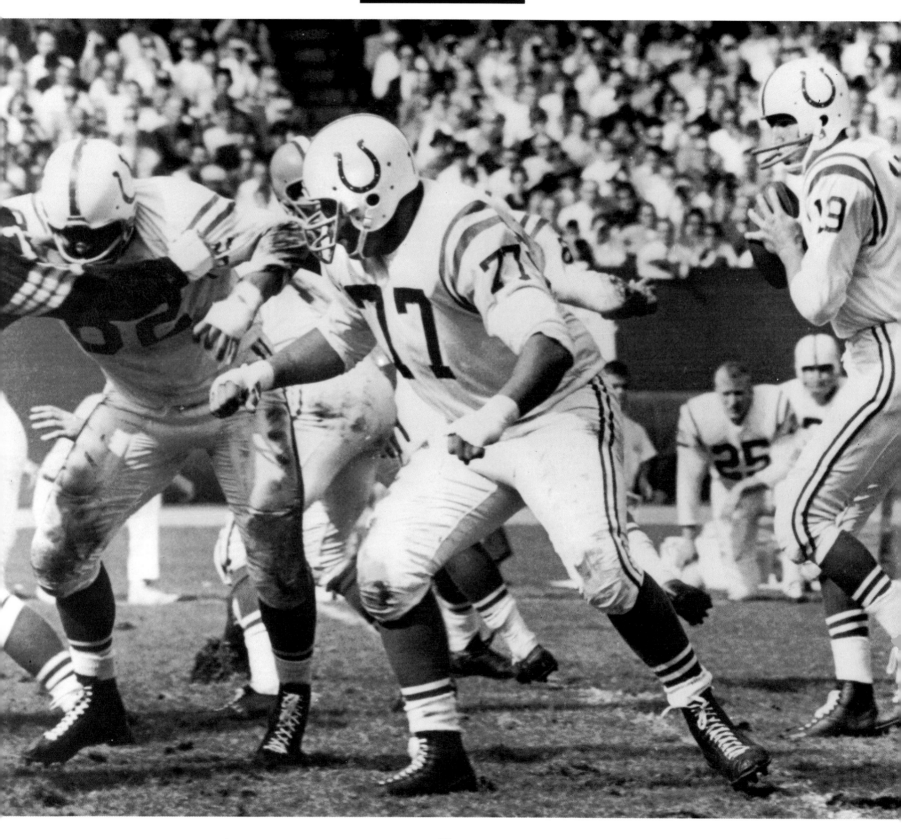

*Walter Payton's grip on football has
been nothing short of phenomenal, as his
airborne work (left) against the New
Orleans Saints attests.*

WALTER PAYTON

Why was Walter Payton the most dominant runner in the history of the NFL? How did the Chicago Bears durable halfback manage to carry the ball 3,692 times for 16,193 yards through 1986?

"It's simple," says Chicago trainer Frank Caito, "he's got a big butt."

At 5–foot–11, 202 pounds, Payton was not a big running back, nor was he particularly fast. Durability is another thing, though. Payton's formidable rear not only protected him from some abusive hits, but it allowed him to lift his legs a little higher than the average Bear — or running back, for that matter. He therefore spent more time in the air, less time on the ground, and was less likely to suffer a direct hit from defenders. Payton's high-kicking style sometimes reminded one of a deer in flight.

He is known as "Sweetness" but that's not the handle used by the men who tried to tackle him. Payton was tough. He seemed to relish contact, in the manner of the old two-way players. When running out of bounds, Payton often put his helmet down and drove into an opponent before leaving the field. This kind of enthusiasm carried Payton through many lean years with the Bears; until he reached the age of 30, Payton performed without the aid of talented blocking. He compensated in the weight room, where he was something of a legend. Payton bench presses 390 pounds and can lift more than 600 pounds with his spectacular legs.

It was that way, too, at Jackson State University. Payton scored 464 points there, a NCAA record that included 66 touchdowns, assorted field goals, and extra points. Although Payton served as placekicker and punter too, it was as a running back that he electrified the professional scouts. He gained 3,563 yards in four years, averaging 6.1 yards every time he carried the ball. On draft day in 1975, Chicago, choosing fourth, held its breath. Steve Bartkowski, Randy White, and Ken Huff were taken and the Bears collected Payton and immediately asked him to carry the struggling offense.

After a disappointing debut season (by his lofty standards) Payton won the NFC rushing title in 1976 with 1,390 yards. He would win four more such titles in a row and clear 1,000 yards for six consecutive years. Were it not for the strike-shortened season of 1982, Payton might have gained more than 1,000 yards for 11 years running, through 1986. He beat Jim Brown, O.J. Simpson, and Franco Harris to the 10,000–yard mark and in 1984 broke Brown's career rushing mark of 12,312 yards.

Coach Mike Ditka arrived in Chicago in 1983 and soon Payton's support crew improved. The Bears won 10 games in 1984, then capped a 15–1 season with a triumph in Super Bowl XX. At age 32, Payton gained 1,333 yards in 1986 and remained the focus of the Bears' potent offense. With the addition of several young running backs, Chicago used Payton more sparingly in the 1987 season, after which he retired.

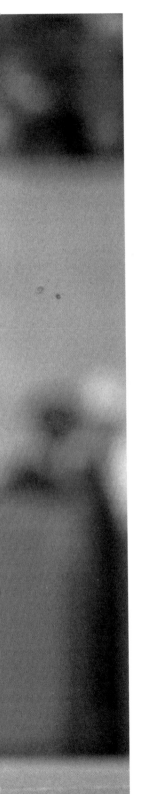

Payton's splay-footed, open-field running is a treat to watch. No one does it better than Payton.

O.J. SIMPSON

O J. Simpson was the first Heisman Trophy winner to be enshrined in the Pro Football Hall of Fame. Many people, Jim Brown notwithstanding, feel Simpson was the game's greatest running back ever. "The Juice" always delivered the goods.

His size (6–foot–1, 212 pounds) wasn't particularly formidable but his speed and field vision were remarkable. Simpson was a world-class sprinter who seemed to see holes before they opened up. His ability to accelerate and change direction quickly once through the hole made Simpson a difficult man to bring down. For his career, Simpson gained 11,236 yards rushing, along with 203 receptions and 70 touchdowns.

Those numbers fail to convey the magnitude of Simpson's achievement, because many of his greatest moments were produced in a relative vacuum. After joining the Buffalo Bills in 1969, (they had earned the right to draft him first overall by finishing 1–12–1 the year before) the Bills lost 33 of 42 games over the next three seasons while Simpson suffered. Slowly, a support system was organized. In 1972, Simpson gained 1,251 yards and won his first NFL rushing title.

A year later, Simpson made history by becoming the first man to run the ball more than 2,000 yards in a single season. Simpson cleared 100 yards in 11 of 14 games and finished with 2,003 yards — a record that would stand until Eric Dickerson of the Los Angeles Rams broke it during the 16 game 1984 season. Simpson finished the season in a flurry, gaining 219 yards against New England, then closing the year with a 200–yard effort against the New York Jets. That was the game Simpson broke Brown's previous single-season record of 1,863.

While historically not a durable player, Simpson was one of the best late-game running backs ever — which partly accounts for his record of six games with more than 200 yards rushing. Though Simpson played behind a good offensive line in his remaining years with the Bills, all those early hits took their toll. Simpson spent his last season, 1978, with San Francisco, where he was born 31 years earlier. At that point, Simpson's great talents had eroded. Fortunately, the memories remain.

In a game against Pittsburgh in 1975, Simpson received a tribute that nearly matched his brilliance. The halfback had shredded the "Steel Curtain" for 227 yards as the Bills forged a 30–21 upset. Steelers defensive end Dwight White knew he had seen a legend that day. "He leaps, he soars, he twists and turns and flies through the air," White said. "He's the greatest I ever saw."

O.J. Simpson, here hurdling the New York Giants' fallen Beasley Reece, was graceful in the air and on the ground.

It was in 1973 that Simpson elevated running to an art form. He gained 219 yards against the New England Patriots (far right), then blistered the New York Jets (right), for 200 more. The total was 2,003 yards — an impossible record at the time.

*Fran Tarkenton proved you didn't have
to be a strapping 6-4, 210-pounder to
play quarterback in the NFL. He defined
the term "scrambler."*

FRAN TARKENTON

He wasn't built along the classic lines of a prototypical quarter-back — Fran Tarkenton was 6 feet tall and weighed 185 pounds, maybe — and his right arm was suspect. No one, however, questioned his determination. In a career that spanned 18 years, Tarkenton became the most productive quarterback in football history.

Tarkenton leads all NFL passers in the four meaningful career statistics: 6,467 attempts, 3,686 completions, 47,003 yards, and 342 touchdowns. As completely dominant as these numbers are,

Tarkenton's greatest contribution to football was in a different arena: He was the original scrambler. As the passing game took hold in the NFL through the 1950s, quarterbacks learned to drop back five to seven steps into the protective pocket of blockers. From that vantage point, they could look over the defense and choose the best target. Tarkenton changed all that. And it was hardly divine inspiration — he had no other choice.

In 1961, Tarkenton arrived in Minnesota after four years at the University of Georgia. The Vikings were a first year expansion team and had few quality players. This was especially true of the offensive line, and though Tarkenton had run frequently at Georgia, he found himself under duress on a regular basis in Minnesota. Invariably, Tarkenton would feel the pressure of onrushing linemen and scramble out of the pocket. This did two things. First, Tarkenton avoided a quarterback sack and, second, he stretched defenses to the breaking point. Tarkenton bought time for his receivers, who adjusted their pass routes and often broke into the clear.

The Vikings lost all five of their pre-season games in 1961 by a total of 66 points and met Chicago in their regular season debut. The result was shocking. Tarkenton threw four touchdown passes and eluded the Bears for most of the 37–13 game won by Minnesota. Soon his scrambling became a trademark. Tarkenton's nimble feet and terrific peripheral vision made him very difficult to pin down and Tarkenton would finish his career with 3,674 rushing yards — another record for NFL quarterbacks.

Tarkenton threw for 1,997 yards his rookie season and cleared 2,000 yards for each of the next 15 years, another all-time mark. He played with Minnesota for six seasons, until 1967, when he was traded to the New York Giants for four draft choices. He played there for five years until 1972, when the Vikings shipped five players back to the Giants for him. Tarkenton played in Minnesota for seven more seasons before retiring in 1978.

He was named to play in the Pro Bowl nine different times and took the Vikings to three different Super Bowls. Typically, he was criticized for failing to lead Minnesota to victory. It was always that way with Tarkenton. He didn't rifle the ball from the comfort of the pocket in the manner of Joe Namath or Johnny Unitas, but he got results. The bottom line is hard to dispute.

Tarkenton could run with the ball, but he had fair success heaving it, too. In fact, no one in NFL history threw the football more times, for more yards, or more touchdowns than Fran Tarkenton.

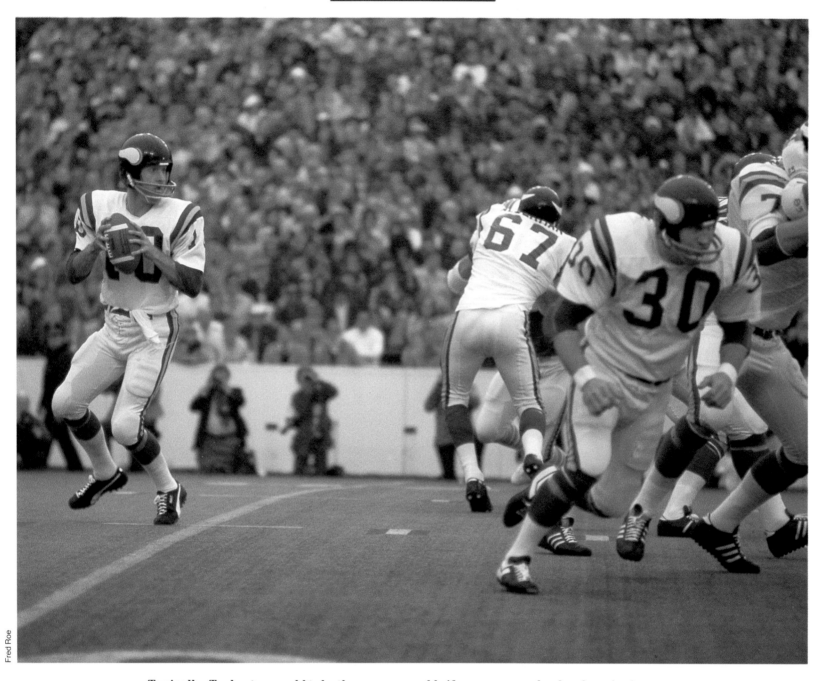

Fred Roe

Typically, Tarkenton would take the snap, scramble if necessary, and unleash a winning pass.

CHARLEY TAYLOR

He had been an All-America running back at Arizona State and in 1964 Charley Taylor was named the NFL's Rookie of the Year. It was almost too easy; Taylor set a league record for running backs with 52 pass receptions. Even with that compelling evidence, the Washington Redskins were a year away from recognizing Taylor's true calling.

At 6–foot–3, 210 pounds, Taylor was big enough to take punishing hits at the line of scrimmage. At the same time, he was swift and deft enough to elude defensive backs and make spectacular catches. Otto Graham, the great Hall of Fame quarterback, understood that the latter ability was the greatest of Taylor's blessings and when Graham became the head coach in 1966, Taylor was moved exclusively to split end. Quarterback Sonny Jurgensen, who had arrived in 1964, was delighted.

In 1966, Taylor led the NFL with 72 catches, worth 1,119 yards. Suddenly, the Redskins were just about impossible to stop. On November 27, they defeated the New York Giants, 72–41, in a game that set a league record for points scored. In 1967, Taylor again led the NFL in receptions with 70 — for 990 yards. It was an incredible year for the Redskins' offense: Jurgensen set league records for attempts, completions, and yards; Jerry Smith finished second behind Taylor in catches and Bobby Mitchell was fourth.

Taylor caught 50 or more passes in a season seven different times, which tied a record. In the course of his 13-year career, Taylor was voted to the Pro Bowl eight times. On December 21, 1975, Taylor became the NFL's all-time leading receiver in the season's last game against Philadelphia. His 634th catch vaulted him past New York's Don Maynard. An injury forced Taylor to miss the 1976 season, but he returned for one final effort in 1977. He finished with 649 catches, worth 9,110 yards and 79 touchdowns. Overall, Taylor amassed 10,883 yards and 90 touchdowns.

Charlie Joiner (Houston, Cincinnati, San Diego) eventually broke Taylor's record, but the old Redskin is getting even in his own way. After retiring in 1978, Taylor joined the Washington scouting staff. When Joe Gibbs became head coach in 1981, he asked Taylor to become one of his assistants. Under Taylor's guidance Charlie Brown became a Pro Bowl receiver in 1982. Two years later, Art Monk set a NFL record with 106 catches. In 1985, Taylor coached the league's best pass-catching tandem: Monk and Gary Clark combined for 163 catches.

Washington's Charley Taylor was just about the perfect wide receiver. Here, he hauls one in behind Dallas defensive back Mel Renfro.

He had size, he had speed, and he was incredibly consistent: Taylor caught 50 or more passes in seven different seasons.

LAWRENCE TAYLOR

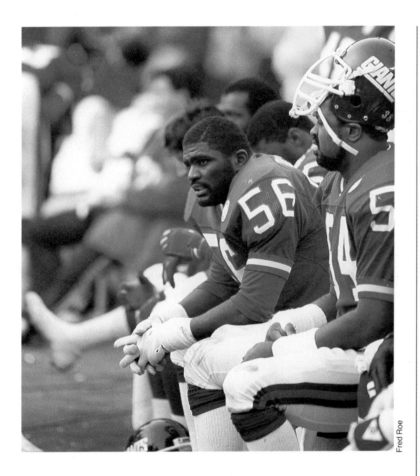

Fred Roe

No one epitomizes the modern game of football — in all its wicked speed and brutal glory — quite like Lawrence Taylor. When his career ends, he will probably be described as the best linebacker in history.

At 6–foot–3, 250 pounds, the Giants' enforcer is bigger and faster than most of the men he pursues on the field. Quarterbacks, however, are his favorite sport. In the first six years of his career, through 1986, Taylor has registered a staggering 71 sacks.

Taylor lives his life on the edge and plays football the same way. "I guess I'm just a plain, wild dude," Taylor says. "I don't really care what other people expect of me, or what I'm supposed to do. I do it my way and try to get the job done that way."

Taylor's success is based on this unsurpassed spirit. "He is completely reckless," says one Giants' assistant coach. "I have never seen a player sell out so completely to make a play. He doesn't care what the consequences are — to his body, or anybody else's."

Taylor is presently the NFL's most intimidating player. No one else is even close. Quarterbacks, concerned for their own safety, monitor his progress as they drift back to pass. Philadelphia's Ron Jaworski admits Taylor dominates his darkest nightmares. And Washington's Joe Theismann has a true life tale of Taylor's breathless qualities of mayhem: Crashing the line of scrimmage in a 1985 game, Taylor broke Theismann's leg and ended his brilliant career.

Even a terrific college career didn't prepare the NFL for Taylor's impact. He was a consensus All-America at the University of North Carolina, sacking quarterbacks 16 times his senior year. The New Orleans Saints drafted first in 1981, but they opted for running back George Rogers. The Giants, who had suffered a dismal 4–12 1980 season, allowing 425 points, chose Taylor. In his first training camp scrimmage, Taylor produced four quarterback sacks and a fumble recovery. Playing Chicago in his first preseason game, Taylor made 10 solo tackles, adding two sacks and another fumble recovery. Taylor finished the regular season with 9 1/2 sacks and led the team with 133 tackles. More importantly, the Giants finished 9–7 and made the playoffs for the first time in 18 years. Their defense also allowed 168 fewer points.

Taylor managed 7 1/2 sacks in the strike-shortened 1982 season, then registered totals of 9, 11 1/2, and 13 1/2 before the Giants turned him loose in 1986. Previously, Taylor had played right outside linebacker, but the Giants altered their defense slightly and effectively made him a stand-up defensive end. By doubling Taylor's pass-rushing opportunities, the Giants forced opponents to offer a variety of double and triple team blocking packages more often. When Taylor didn't get to the quarterback, someone else usually did.

In 1986, the Giants won the last 12 games of the season and thrashed the Denver Broncos 39–20 in Super Bowl XXI. Though quarterback Phil Simms was named the game's Most Valuable Player, it was Taylor who led the Giants to football's throne from the depths of mediocrity. At the age of 28, some observers already insist he is the game's greatest player ever.

Fred Roe

JOHNNY UNITAS

Johnny Unitas could read defenses, run if he had to, and hit receivers, systematically dismantling the opposition.

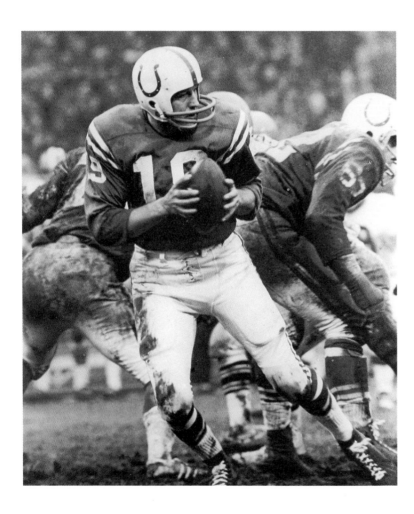

When George Shaw went down with an injury against the Chicago Bears in the fourth game of the 1966 season, Unitas got his big break. The first pass he threw, though, was intercepted by J.D. Caroline and returned for a touchdown. Critics wondered what a sandlot quarterback was doing in the big leagues.

Unitas, of course, went on to set 22 different NFL records and became one of the greatest quarterbacks in history. In 18 years, Unitas attempted 5,186 passes and completed 2,830 of them for 40,239 yards and 290 touchdowns — all records until Fran Tarkenton broke them in the late 1960s. Unitas threw over 300 yards in 26 different games, and during one stretch of his career completed touchdown passes in 47 consecutive games.

Unitas, at 6-foot-1, 196 pounds, had only an adequate arm and decent footspeed. But he was one of the smartest football players ever. It was Unitas' leadership ability, presence under pressure, and touch on difficult passes that separated him from the rest. He rarely called the obvious play, which made defending the Colts difficult during his tenure. He was a master of the two-minute drill and perhaps the most dangerous passer into the end zone. Unitas was also a master of the screen pass, a delicate art in a brutal game.

Three different times Unitas was named the NFL's Most Valuable Player, as well as being named MVP in three of the 10 Pro Bowls he appeared in. Unitas was, in every way, a championship player. He led the Colts to NFL titles in 1958 and 1959 and would later set post-season records for highest completion percentage (62.9) and most yards gained in championship play (1,177).

Although Unitas, at age 36, quarterbacked the Colts to victory in Super Bowl V in 1970, it was an earlier game that season which best captured his determination and spirit. The Chicago Bears led 17–0 midway through the first quarter on November 29; Unitas had thrown three interceptions and seen teammates drop his other three pass attempts. With several perfect calls though, Unitas drove the Colts 80 yards for a touchdown in the second quarter. And with one minute left in the first half, Unitas completed a critical fourth-and-three pass to Eddie Hinton, following with a scoring pass to Roy Jefferson. Later, trailing 20–14 with five minutes to play, Unitas hit tight end John Mackey on consecutive plays of 22 yards and then 54 yards for a touchdown. Baltimore won 21–20 when Unitas ran the clock out. The Colts won their last three regular season games and swept through the playoffs. Not bad for a $6-a-game quarterback.

Forgive the Pittsburgh Steelers. They may have waived an undistinguished Louisville quarterback back in 1955, but the rest of the NFL passed on him, too.

Johnny Unitas was a ninth round pick of the Steelers and he was waived from training camp before he even had a chance to throw a pass under game conditions. Unitas signed on with a semipro team in the Pittsburgh area called the Bloomfield Rams, earning $6 per game for playing on a field covered with broken bottles and stones. After the season, Baltimore Colts' coach Weeb Ewbank received a letter from a Bloomfield fan that spoke highly of the Rams' first-year quarterback. The following summer Unitas was invited to the Colts' camp and given a contract worth $7,000.

Johnny Unitas set 22 different NFL records, including one that may never be broken: A Joe DiMaggio-like series of 47 consecutive games with at least one touchdown pass. Not bad for a ninth-round draft choice.

Fred Roe

THE GREATEST GAMES

They come in different guises, these games from football's great trunk of history.

In it is the 1940 National Football League championship game, a searing 73–0 triumph for the Chicago Bears over the Washington Redskins. There is the 1981 sudden-death marathon between the San Diego Chargers and Miami Dolphins, a 1,036–yard contest decided by Rolf Benirschke's 29–yard field goal with 13:52 elapsed in overtime. Consider Super Bowl XX, the Chicago Bears' 46–10 dismantling of the New England Patriots. It was played in the climate controlled environs of the Louisiana Superdome in New Orleans. The 1934 NFL championship game unfolded on a sheet of ice at the Polo Grounds.

Broadway Joe Namath and his rifle arm led the New York Jets to one of the greatest upsets of all time over the Baltimore Colts, 16–7, in Super Bowl III. Those same Colts had won an important game in 1965 without a quarterback at all when running back Tom Matte, reading the plays from a card taped to his wrist, pushed the Colts to an inspired victory over the Los Angeles Rams.

Many people who witnessed the 1958 NFL championship game, a 23–17 Baltimore win over the New York Giants in sudden-death overtime, contend it was the greatest game in football history. Who is to say?

In 1968, the New York Jets were leading the Los Angeles Raiders 32–29 with time running out when NBC switched most of the nation to the *Heidi* children's special. The Raiders scored two last minute touchdowns and the barrage of angry calls that ensued spoke volumes about the growing influence of football.

The games that follow all are significant in the history of football. Many of these inspiring contests featured some of the game's biggest names. Others were technically less important, yet undeniably compelling. All were great.

73

Although Chicago's Bill Osmanski didn't get the best of this play, the Bears still decimated the Washington Redskins in the 1940 NFL championship game.

THE BIG BLOWOUT

DECEMBER 8, 1940

NFL CHAMPIONSHIP GAME

CHICAGO 73, WASHINGTON 0

Only three weeks earlier, the Chicago Bears had lost a 7–3 game to the Washington Redskins. On the game's last play, Bears' quarterback Sid Luckman drilled the ball to teammate Bill Osmanski in the end zone but it bounced off his chest — because, the Bears maintained later, Washington defender Frank Filchock had pinned Osmanski's hands at his side. The Redskins dismissed the Bears as sore losers and said so for the benefit of newspaper writers.

On December 8, Chicago was ready for their rematch in the NFL championship game. Coach George Halas had lined the dressing room walls with newspapers bearing Washington's haughty comments after their victory three weeks earlier. No one, not even Papa Bear, who would finish his NFL coaching career with a record 321 victories, was prepared for what followed: a 73–0 victory that for sheer majesty has never been approached.

Halas, always looking for an edge, asked Stanford coach Clark Shaughnessy to help the Bears in their pre-game preparations. Shaughnessy, a film expert, broke down the Redskins' defensive tendencies in their previous meeting with the Bears and, along with Halas, devised ways to defeat those strategies. There were lectures, written exams and enough rehash of that 7–3 loss that the Bears couldn't wait to step on the field in Washington.

The Bears' first play, a short pitch from Luckman to George McAfee, was designed to test the Redskins defense. Sure enough, they were playing the same defense and McAfee gained eight yards between right guard and tackle. The next play, a spinning handoff to Osmanski, was executed perfectly. George Wilson's block sprung Osmanski for a 68–yard touchdown — just 55 seconds into the game.

Max Krause took the ensuing kickoff back to the Chicago 40–yard line and quarterback Sammy Baugh moved Washington another 15 yards before Bob Masterson's 32–yard field goal missed. Eighty yards and 17 plays later, Luckman was sneaking over from the 1–yard line and the lead was 14–0. After Joe Maniaci's 42–yard run following a fullback lateral play, the score was 21–0. Luckman found end Ken Kavanaugh with a 30–yard touchdown pass to push the halftime lead to 28–0.

And then Halas told the Bears in their dressing room that the Redskins had called them a first half team only three weeks earlier.

On the second play of the second half, Hampton Pool intercepted Baugh's short pass in the flat and ran it in for a 15–yard touchdown. When Baugh's fourth–and-20 pass from his own 34–yard line fell incomplete the rout was on. Even rookie quarterback Sollie Sherman couldn't help but drive the Bears nine plays and 58 yards for another touchdown. When Gary Famiglietti scored minutes later, the referee asked the Bears to eschew the extra point — too many footballs had been kicked into the stands and only a few battered practice balls were left. Naturally, the conversion pass from Sherman to Maniaci was good. Harry Clark scored after the Bears' eighth interception of the game and became the only player to score twice. Ten different players scored Chicago's 11 touchdowns and all 33 players on the roster saw action.

As a result of that stunning scoring display, the T-formation employed by the Bears became universally accepted. So did the notion that this 1940 Bears team was among the greatest in football history.

(above) In more ways than one the Los Angeles Rams were trapped by the Cleveland Browns in the 1950 championship game. (right) Cleveland quarterback Otto Graham ran, and passed, the Browns to a 30-28 victory that sent coaches scurrying to redesign their teams.

THE GREAT DEBATE IS SETTLED

DECEMBER 24, 1950
NFL CHAMPIONSHIP GAME
CLEVELAND 30, LOS ANGELES
RAMS 28

The United States Football League and the old American Football League had nothing on the All-America Football Conference. No, the USFL (which officially folded in 1986) and the AFL (absorbed by the NFL in 1970) were relative newcomers to the business of professional football. The AAFC was itself a spin–off, representing merely the fourth effort by a league to challenge the incumbent NFL in the first 30 years of its existence.

From 1946–49, the AAFC gave the NFL a run for its money. Attendance over that period actually slightly outpaced the NFL's, probably a reaction to the name players the new league attracted. The AAFC signed 40 of the 1946 College All-Star Team's 66 members and induced more than 100 former NFL stars to join after service in the U.S. armed forces.

The quality of play seemed comparable, but no one knew for sure because the champions of the rival leagues didn't play each other. Although the Cleveland Browns had won all four AAFC championships and put together a ludicrously successful 51–4–3 record, the debate raged as to whether they would be able to make it in the NFL. In 1950, the NFL absorbed the Cleveland franchise (as well as the teams in San Francisco and Baltimore), which meant the Browns would now face other NFL teams. The great debate would soon be over.

In an immediate effort to see which league had the best champion, NFL commissioner Bert Bell scheduled the Browns against the Philadelphia Eagles in the 1950 season opener. The Eagles, winners of two consecutive league titles — they dusted the Chicago Cardinals 7–0 in the 1948 final and came back a year later to defeat the Los Angeles Rams 14–0 — were six point favorites in a match–up the newspapers were calling "the most talked-about game in NFL history."

Cleveland shocked many people and won in brutal fashion, closing out Philadelphia 35–10. But this was only the regular season. The Browns finished 10–2 before defeating the New York Giants 8–3 in a divisional playoff game. The championship game, against the Los Angeles Rams team that had pulled out of Cleveland just before the Browns arrived, was a telling blow for the old AAFC.

Using the free substitution rule that had been implemented that year, Cleveland coach Paul Brown unleashed quarterback Otto Graham and a new wave passing game that forever changed the way football men drew X's and O's. Still, the Rams were winning the battle 28–27 in the fourth quarter when placekicker Lou Groza, the goat of the game so far, was given a chance to win it. Groza had missed an extra point earlier, which explained the uneven score. This time Groza was on target and he converted a 16–yard field goal with 28 seconds left in the game.

The Browns were 30–28 winners and went on to appear in the next four championship games. The NFL had not only weathered the challenge of another new league, it had grown stronger.

The immortal 16-Power Play: Baltimore Colts fullback Alan Ameche comes to earth in the end zone with Sam Huff and Jim Patton (20) wrapped around him. With gritty playing like this, Baltimore toughed-out a sudden death win over the New York Giants in the 1958 championship game.

THE GREATEST GAME EVER?

DECEMBER 28, 1958

NFL CHAMPIONSHIP GAME

BALTIMORE 23, NEW YORK

GIANTS 17

It was the first NFL championship game to be decided in sudden-death overtime and to this day remains the last name in unparalleled excitement. The 1958 championship game had everything: a handful of future Hall of Famers, a marvelously gripping setting at Yankee Stadium, and a drama that still burns in the hearts of the men who participated in it.

The Cleveland Browns *should* have lined up opposite Baltimore in the final. They needed only a tie in the regular season finale against the Giants to capture the conference championship, but placekicker Pat Summerall's last second field goal of indeterminate length (some claim it was 52 yards) through a blizzard forced a playoff game. The Giants beat Cleveland 10–0 this time and entered the final game against Baltimore as the favorite.

The Colts had clinched the Western Conference title in the season's 10th game and finished the season with losses to the Los Angeles Rams and San Francisco 49ers. Still, they had Johnny Unitas at quarterback.

Earlier in the season, Baltimore had lost a 24–21 game to the Giants on a Summerall field goal and on this cold day Summerall gave the Giants a short–lived 3–0 lead with two minutes left in the first quarter. Frank Gifford's fumble — the first of three in the second quarter — gave Baltimore the ball on the Giants 20–yard line. Six straight running plays, the last from two yards out by fullback Alan Ameche, gave the Colts a 7–3 lead. Then Gifford ended a Giants drive with a fumble on the Baltimore 14–yard line. A pass from Unitas to Raymond Berry made the score 14–3.

The Colts appeared to have the game won early in the third quarter when they found themselves with first-and-goal at the Giants 3–yard line. Three times Baltimore's powerful Ameche carried the ball up the middle and three times the Giants' defense stopped him. It was fourth-and-goal at the 1 and the Colts elected to break the game open, which they very nearly did — at their own expense. Unitas sent Ameche wide to take advantage of the Giants bunched defense, but the Giants saw the play coming and decked him for a four yard loss.

On third–and–2 from the Giants 13, quarterback Charlie Conerly reached Kyle Rote with a long pass, but he fumbled. Teammate Alex Webster picked it up and raced to the Baltimore 1–yard line. The play went 86 yards and Mel Triplett's subsequent touchdown dive narrowed the score to 14–10. Conerly's 15–yard pass to Gifford gave the Giants a 17–14 lead. With 1:56 left, the Colts began a drive from their own 14–yard line. Unitas, with Berry as his primary target, moved Baltimore into position for Steve Myrha's 20–yard field goal with seven seconds left in regulation. The score was 17–17 when time ran out.

The Giants' first extra possession resulted in a Don Chandler punt and Baltimore took over on its own 20–yard line. Unitas presided over a creative drive, finding, variously, Ameche, Lenny Moore, and Berry. Eventually, Ameche took a handoff from Unitas at the 1–yard line. The play was the Colts' 16–Power Play and Moore made a terrific block off right tackle, allowing Ameche to score standing up. The first hands to touch him were those of the Baltimore fans who crashed out of the stands to mob Ameche. Giants lay strewn around the end zone.

And so, 8:15 into sudden-death overtime, the greatest football game in history was over.

A TEAM WITHOUT A QUARTERBACK

DECEMBER 19, 1965
BALTIMORE 20, LOS ANGELES
RAMS 14

The Baltimore Colts had one game remaining in the 1965 regular season — a crucial contest with the Los Angeles Rams that would determine if they would be a playoff team — and no one to call the signals. Two weeks earlier, quarterback Johnny Unitas had been lost when two Chicago Bears combined to snap the ligaments in his knee. The following week, backup signal caller Gary Cuozzo suffered a shoulder separation.

Now coach Don Shula had only two men left who could play the position: defensive back Bobby Boyd, who had played quarterback at Oklahoma, and running back Tom Matte, a former quarterback at Ohio State. Both players had directed run-oriented offenses and weren't familiar with the drop-back style employed by Unitas and Cuozzo. Matte, based on his knowledge of the Colts offense, was Shula's choice. At a team meeting, Shula told the players that sound defense could defeat the Rams. Then he unveiled Matte as his quarterback. At practice, the defensive linemen began laughing when Matte, in his high pitched voice, started calling signals at the line of scrimmage.

As the week progressed, Matte couldn't seem to grasp the Colts newly simplified offense — or the snaps from center, for that matter. So two days before the game, Baltimore picked up veteran quarterback Ed Brown on waivers from Pittsburgh. Shula prepared a different offensive plan for both of them. Yet Brown looked shaky in his first practice with the Colts and Matte missed dinner with a temperature and signs of the flu. Shula began to worry. When Matte failed to complete a pass in the team's pre-game practice, worry gave way to terror.

"It was," Shula says, "without a doubt the flattest practice I have ever been associated with as a coach or player. Generally, the pre-game practice is a good indicator as to what to expect when the game starts. But, in this instance, I couldn't have been more wrong."

The Colts' defense contained Rams quarterback Roman Gabriel for much of the first half. With Matte taking the bulk of the snaps — and the basic plays taped to his wrist for easy reference — Baltimore took a 3–0 lead on Lou Michael's 50–yard field goal. Two plays after a fumble recovery, the Colts scored a touchdown when Lenny Moore beat a Los Angeles blitz with a 28–yard off-tackle run. The 10–0 lead evaporated when Gabriel reached Tommy McDonald with a 10–yard touchdown late in the second quarter and a 30–yard strike to Jack Snow in the third quarter.

Shula sent Brown into the game on third-and–6 early in the fourth quarter. He hit tight end John Mackey with a short pass over the middle that split the Rams' zone for a 68–yard touchdown. Then Matte took over on the next series and burned the Rams with a variety of quarterback-keepers. He ran down the clock and moved the Colts into field goal position. Michael's 23–yard field goal gave Baltimore its unlikely victory.

A week later, Matte was the quarterback again in a game against the Packers for the Western Division title. Green Bay won on a disputed field 13:39 into sudden-death overtime, but Matte and the Colts had given football another legendary performance.

Green Bay quarterback Bart Starr lies on the frozen field after scoring from the 1-yard line. It was a dramatic ending to one of football's greatest games.

THE ICE BOWL

JANUARY 1, 1967
GREEN BAY 21, DALLAS 17

Here they were again, the NFL's two best teams locked in grim combat with the championship on the line. A year earlier, the Green Bay Packers had prevailed 34–27 at the Cotton Bowl in Dallas. Quarterback Bart Starr had thrown four touchdown passes, but it was defensive back Tom Brown who saved the game with an interception of Don Meredith's fourth down pass from the Green Bay 2–yard line.

This year, though, the game took on additional significance, because during the 1966 off-season, the NFL merged with the American Football League. To the league winners went a berth in the first Super Bowl. In the new alignment, the Cowboys rolled through the season 9–5 and humbled Cleveland 52–14 in the first round of the playoffs. The Packers, 12–2 over the regular season, were looking for their third straight league title and a spot in the first Super Bowl.

The deciding contest became known as "The Ice Bowl." The temperature that day at Green Bay's Lambeau Field was 16

degrees below zero. Just as they had in 1966, the Packers jumped out to a 14–0 first quarter lead. Starr hit Boyd Dowler with scoring passes of 8 and 46 yards before the Cowboys seemed to warm to their considerable task.

Defensive end George Andrie recovered a Starr fumble and carried it seven yards into the end zone to cut the score to 14–7 in the second quarter. Minutes later, Danny Villanueva's 21–yard field goal cut the margin to 14–10. Meredith would only pass for 50 yards in the game, with the weather making it nearly impossible for him to throw the ball accurately. It was Dan Reeves who seemingly won the game in the fourth quarter with a 58–yard scoring heave to Lance Rentzel. The Cowboys led, 17–14.

The 50,861 shivering fans in the stands grew silent. There was little time left and the Packers hadn't made an appreciable dent in the Dallas defense for most of three quarters. Starr slowly roused Green Bay and drove his team down the field. Eleven plays and 67 yards took him to the Dallas 1–yard line. With 13 seconds left in the game and no time outs remaining, Starr chose to follow his heart and his offensive line. Although tackle Forrest Gregg and center Jim Ringo had gone to the Pro Bowl 16 times between them, Starr opted to sneak behind guard Jerry Kramer. When he emerged from the heap in the end zone, Starr and the Packers had won their fifth NFL title in seven years.

Super Bowl I, a grinding 35–10 Green Bay victory over the Kansas City Chiefs two weeks later in sunny Los Angeles, was almost anticlimactic.

That's Raider Charlie Smith scoring on a 43-yard pass with 42 seconds left on the clock — a play the television audience wouldn't see, thanks to Heidi.

THE HEIDI BOWL

NOVEMBER 17, 1968
OAKLAND 43, NEW YORK JETS 32

She may have had a charming, Tyrolian grace about her, but what was a nice girl with blonde braids doing in the middle of an ugly game like this? That was the question much of America asked Monday morning, November 18 as *Heidi* had became part of the football fan's working vocabulary in a series of bizarre events.

The Oakland Raiders and New York Jets were easily the class of the AFL in 1968 and the National Broadcasting Company was delighted to deliver the November 17 game from Oakland's County Coliseum to the nation's homes. From the beginning it was a hard fought game between two teams hungry for the championship. There had been bad blood between them since Oakland defensive end Ben Davidson had broken the cheekbone of Jets quaterback Joe Namath the year before. Today there was a penalty on the game's opening kickoff and then things degenerated.

The Raiders escaped the first half with a 14–12 lead — the second quarter had required 49 minutes and the Jets alone were called for seven penalties in the first half. After the Jets took a brief 19–14 lead, Oakland scored on a long drive that saw New York safety Jim Hudson thrown out of the game for unsportsman-like conduct. The Jets rallied, though, when Namath drove them 97 yards for a touchdown and placekicker Jim Turner added a 19–yard field goal.

With 3:55 left on the clock, Oakland quarterback Daryle Lamonica threw a 22–yard touchdown pass to Fred Biletnikoff. That tied the score at 29–all. The Jets seemed to have the game won when Turner's 26–yard field goal split the uprights with 1:05 remaining, giving them a 32–29 lead. Because of all the mayhem, the game was running late — and at 7:10 p.m. Eastern time, NBC made a fateful decision.

Heidi, a special children's movie, had been scheduled to follow the football game at 7 p.m. With a Jets' victory all but assured, NBC switched to *Heidi*. Millions of viewers in the east and midwest never saw the dramatic ending, missing two improbable touchdowns by the Raiders in the game's final 50 seconds. First, Lamonica moved Oakland 78 yards in two plays. His 43–yard pass to running back Charles Smith gave them a 36–32 lead. Then, on George Blanda's subsequent kickoff, Preston Ridlehuber carried a fumble two yards into the end zone.

Oakland won the game, 43–32, and the NBC switchboard was buried by thousands of calls and eventually broke down under the strain. The New York Police Department, city newspapers, and the Jets offices on Long Island were besieged with calls.

It would be the only loss in the season's last 11 games for the Jets. The Raiders, 1967's AFL champs, would fall to the eventual winners of Super Bowl III five weeks later in the championship game, 27–23, at Shea Stadium. *Heidi* was not present.

Although his knees didn't work very well, Joe Namath's mouth ran overtime. He promised a victory over the Baltimore Colts in Super Bowl III and then delivered.

NAMATH DELIVERS

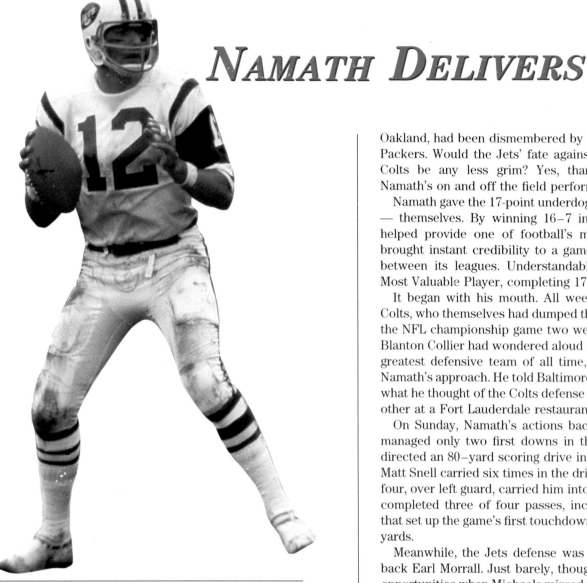

JANUARY 12, 1969
SUPER BOWL III
NEW YORK JETS 16, BALTIMORE 7

Oakland, had been dismembered by Vince Lombardi's Green Bay Packers. Would the Jets' fate against the NFL's 15–1 Baltimore Colts be any less grim? Yes, thanks almost entirely to Joe Namath's on and off the field performances.

Namath gave the 17-point underdog Jets something to believe in — themselves. By winning 16–7 in the Orange Bowl, Namath helped provide one of football's most memorable upsets and brought instant credibility to a game desperately seeking parity between its leagues. Understandably, Namath was named the Most Valuable Player, completing 17 of 28 passes for 206 yards.

It began with his mouth. All week long, Namath trashed the Colts, who themselves had dumped the Cleveland Browns 34–0 in the NFL championship game two weeks earlier. Cleveland coach Blanton Collier had wondered aloud if Don Shula's Colts were the greatest defensive team of all time, but there was little awe in Namath's approach. He told Baltimore defensive end Lou Michaels what he thought of the Colts defense when they bumped into each other at a Fort Lauderdale restaurant a week before the game.

On Sunday, Namath's actions backed up his hubris. The Jets managed only two first downs in the first quarter, but Namath directed an 80–yard scoring drive in the second period. Fullback Matt Snell carried six times in the drive, gaining 35 yards. The last four, over left guard, carried him into the Colts end zone. Namath completed three of four passes, including a 12–yarder to Snell that set up the game's first touchdown. Snell would finish with 121 yards.

Meanwhile, the Jets defense was handling Baltimore quarterback Earl Morrall. Just barely, though. The Colts missed scoring opportunities when Michaels missed field goals of 27 and 46 yards. Three possessions ended in interceptions — all deep in Jets territory.

Placekicker Jim Turner added three field goals in the second half, modest efforts of 32, 30, and 9 yards that underlined the Jets' steady offense. With 13:10 left, the Jets led, 16–0. Johnny Unitas, who missed most of the season with a sore elbow, had replaced Morrall midway through the third quarter but cornerback Randy Beverly's second interception of the game, in the Jets end zone, prevented the Colts from drawing closer. Finally, with 3:29 left on the clock, Unitas drove Baltimore into the end zone. Fullback Jerry Hill scored from one yard out, but the Jets' defense would not lapse again.

The game ball didn't go to Namath or Snell or Beverly — the Jets voted to award it to the AFL.

With apologies to Yogi Berra (and the English language), this one might have been over before it was over.

"I guarantee that we are going to win the Super Bowl game," quarterback Joe Namath told those attending an awards banquet in the Miami area in the week before Super Bowl III. Plainly, Namath was talking through his New York Jets helmet. In two previous Super Bowls, the AFL champions, Kansas City and

Pittsburgh Steelers quarterback Terry Bradshaw threw a record four touchdowns in the Steelers Super Bowl XIII victory over Dallas. The last one, an 18-yard toss to Lynn Swann, gave the Steelers an insurmountable 35-17 lead.

THE FIRST SUPER BOWL REMATCH

JANUARY 21, 1979
SUPER BOWL XIII
PITTSBURGH 35, DALLAS 31

Most times, Super Bowls fail to live up to the week-long, season climaxing hype that precedes them. The contest noted here, however, is perhaps the only exception, a historical aberration that was as good as its name: Super Bowl XIII, truly a super contest.

The Steelers had beaten the Cowboys 21–17 three years earlier for their second consecutive world championship, and now the two met at the Orange Bowl in Miami in the first Super Bowl rematch. Dallas, a 27–10 winner over Denver in Super Bowl XII, was trying to make it two in a row.

Just five minutes into the game, Pittsburgh quarterback Terry Bradshaw pump-faked and reached John Stallworth with a 28–yard touchdown pass. The Cowboys tied the game when quarterback Roger Staubach threw a 39–yard pass to Tony Hill and then took the lead when Bradshaw was sacked by Dallas linebacker Thomas "Hollywood" Henderson. Mike Hegman stripped the ball from Bradshaw and ran 37 yards for a touchdown.

On the next series, Pittsburgh gave the ball to running back Franco Harris who gained five yards on two carries. On third-and-five at the Steelers 25–yard line, Bradshaw hit Stallworth on a simple 10–yard out pattern along the right sideline. Stallworth spun and shook off the tackle of cornerback Aaron Kyle, then cut back diagonally across the field between two blocks. He broke another tackle on the way to a 75–yard touchdown that tied John Mackey's Super Bowl record and the game, at 14–14. Bradshaw's 7–yard pass to Rocky Bleier with 26 seconds left in the first half gave Pittsburgh a 21–14 lead.

Dallas closed to 21–17 with a Rafael Septien field goal from 27 yards away, but Pittsburgh exploded for two fourth quarter touchdowns in a span of 19 seconds. Bradshaw, faced with a third-and–9 at the Dallas 22, faked a pitch right to Bleier, pivoted, and handed the ball to Harris. Dallas safety Charlie Waters seemed in perfect position to make the stop but was sealed off by a textbook block inadvertantly made by an official at the line of the scrimmage. With 7:10 left, Pittsburgh led 28–17. And then it was 35–17. Randy White fumbled the ensuing kickoff and the Steelers' Dennis Winston recovered. On first down, Bradshaw hit Lynn Swann with an 18–yard touchdown pass — the fourth of the day for Bradshaw, who completed 17 of 30 passes for 318 yards and would be named the game's Most Valuable Player.

Dallas wasn't impressed. Staubach's 7–yard touch-down pass to tight end Billy Joe DuPree cut the score to 35–24 with 2:23 left. The Cowboys then recovered an onside kick and Staubach rallied them to another touchdown, a 4–yard pass to Butch Johnson. Only when Bleier recovered another onside kick with 17 seconds remaining was Pittsburgh assured of winning.

The Steelers thus became the first team to win three Super Bowls. They would add a fourth a year later with a victory over the Los Angeles Rams. It is a record that has yet to be equaled.

The look on Kellen Winslow's face illustrates the monumental effort it took for the San Diego Chargers to beat the Miami Dolphins in a 1982 playoff game. The tight end caught 13 passes for 166 yards. Several times, he was carried off the field by his teammates.

THE GAME THAT WOULD NOT END

JANUARY 2, 1982

AFC PLAYOFF GAME

SAN DIEGO 41, MIAMI 38

It is a memory that lingers: San Diego tight end Kellen Winslow, exhausted and dehydrated, carried repeatedly from the Orange Bowl field. More than anything else, Winslow symbolized the numbing nature of this epic overtime struggle between the Dolphins and Chargers. He caught 13 passes for 166 yards in a game that required an extra 13:52 to play.

Records fell everywhere. The two teams set a playoff mark for points (79) and total yards (1,036). It was the only game in NFL history in which two quarterbacks passed for more than 400 yards. Six different players produced 100–yard games.

The Dolphins were no strangers to prolonged playoff games. In 1971, Miami outlasted the Kansas City Chiefs 27–24 in a game ended in the second overtime by a 37–yard Garo Yepremian field goal. It was the longest playoff game in NFL history.

Eleven years later, things looked considerably dimmer for the Dolphins. After one quarter, the Chargers led 24–0. Rolf Benirschke had kicked a 32–yard field goal and Wes Chandler returned a punt 56 yards for a touchdown. Chuck Muncie's 1–yard run and Dan Fouts' 8–yard pass to James Brooks gave San Diego a lead that

looked untouchable. The Dolphins' backup quarterback Don Strock was called off the bench to relieve starter David Woodley and they scored 17 unanswered points in the second quarter to make it a game.

So it went for most of the second half. Fouts, who eventually completed 33 of 53 passes for 433 yards and three touchdowns, matched Strock (29–for–43, 403 yards, and four touchdowns) throw for throw. A 12–yard sweep by Tony Nathan on the first play of the fourth quarter gave Miami a 38–31 lead, but Fouts orchestrated an 82–yard drive that culminated with a 9–yard touchdown pass to Brooks with 58 seconds left in regulation.

Blame the placekickers for the game's length. Miami's Uwe von Schamann had a 43–yard field goal blocked on the last play of regulation. Then, nearly six minutes into sudden-death overtime, Benirschke missed a 27–yard field goal attempt. Just over five minutes later, von Schamann's 35–yard kick was blocked.

Finally, Fouts connected with Charlie Joiner (7 catches, 108 yards) for a 39–yard pass play that moved the ball down to Miami's 10–yard line. The Chargers immediately lined up for another field goal attempt. This time, Benirschke's 29–yard kick was good, very good, and San Diego had prevailed. Although it wasn't as long as the 1971 Miami — Kansas City game or Cleveland's two-overtime playoff victory over the New York Jets in 1987, this game had *style*.

Eight days after playing in the torrid crucible of Miami's Orange Bowl, the Chargers lost to the Cincinnati Bengals 27–7 in the coldest AFC playoff game ever — the temperature was minus nine degrees, and the wind-chill factor was minus 59 degrees. All in all, it was a tough post-season for the boys from San Diego.

The Chicago Bears had the best of it on both sides of the ball in Super Bowl XX: Quarterback Jim McMahon became the first signal-caller in Super Bowl history to run for two touchdowns (right), and the defense smothered New England quarterbacks with seven sacks (far right).

THE SUPER BOWL MASSACRE

JANUARY 26, 1986

SUPER BOWL XX

CHICAGO 46, NEW ENGLAND 10

In 1985 the Chicago Bears battered and bruised their way through a 15–1 regular season. Then in the playoffs, where opponents are supposed to be worthy, they torched the New York Giants and Los Angeles Rams by a collective score of 45–0. They then went one better in Super Bowl XX.

It was a 46–10 New Orleans razing of the New England Patriots — undeniable proof that the Bears were one of history's best one season teams.

"The [betting] line could have been 35 points and we would

have covered the spread," mused Chicago defensive tackle Steve McMichael, amid the bedlam in the Bears' locker room. "That must mean we're pretty good."

Well, yes. Chicago's victory margin of 36 points was the largest ever for a Super Bowl; the Bears set 11 Super Bowl records, tied 15 more and then awarded everyone in the organization a game ball.

Patriots' coach Raymond Berry, a steely Hall of Famer who had seen more than a few football games in his time, shook his head. "You stay around this league long enough, sooner or later you're going to have your rear end handed to you," Berry said. "We had it handed to us today."

In a lovely coincidence, the Bears' offense scored 46 points on New England while their 46–Defense played with numbing efficiency. It was a throwback to George Halas' Monsters of the Midway, a back-to-the-future stroke of genius on the part of defensive coordinator Buddy Ryan. No fancy substitutions, (the modern day fashion in the NFL) but 11 players with a single purpose. Versatility was the modus operandi. On occasion, defensive end Richard Dent, later voted the game's Most Valuable Player, lined up as a linebacker; strong safety Dave Duerson often played linebacker as well; linebacker Mike Singletary's quickness allowed the Bears to use him as a safety in pass coverage.

With McMichael and Dan Hampton meeting two Patriots players each at the line of scrimmage, the Bears blitzed all three linebackers up the middle. Dent (1 1/2 quarterback sacks and 2 forced fumbles) and Otis Wilson (2 sacks) did most of the damage. New England's starting quarterback Tony Eason and reliever Steve Grogan spent most of the game dazed and confused, reeling from seven sacks and six turnovers. Chicago permitted only 127 net yards — 7 of them constituting the entire Patriots ground game — and 12 first downs.

For the fifth time that season, the Bears defense outscored an opposing offense. Defensive tackle William 'The Refrigerator' Perry scored a touchdown on a 1–yard run and, wonder of wonders, was on the receiving end of a quarterback sack. Chicago's offense merely took advantage of its bountiful gifts from the defense. Quarterback Jim McMahon completed 12 of 20 passes for 256 yards, wide receiver Willie Gault caught 4 passes for 129 yards and halfback Walter Payton carried 22 times for 61 yards. It was an execution of the ugliest, most grisly kind.

On the day they beat the Patriots, the Bears were the NFC's youngest team. Though they didn't repeat their achievement in the 1986 season — a 14–2 regular-season record would be ended by the Washington Redskins in the playoffs — the exuberance of youth and a city longing for football supremacy were served.

THE MOMENTS

t was the New England Patriots' best sweep ever, the big play they had always been looking for against the dreaded Miami Dolphins.

This December 12, 1982 game had been bitterly waged through a blizzard on the frozen Schaefer Stadium field. It was a scoreless tie when an inmate on a work-release program rode a John Deere 314 tractor into football history, creating one of the sport's greatest moments.

With 4:45 left in the game, New England had worked itself into position to win the game. Placekicker John Smith, who had missed two previous field goal attempts when he slipped in the ice and snow, sized up a 33–yarder. The Patriots had called a time out and coach Ron Meyer was frantically searching the sidelines.

"I was saying, 'Let's get the sweeper out there,'" Meyer said later, "here was a guy who could really help us — but I had to find him. Finally, I spotted him on the 10–yard line and ran down there. I screamed, 'Get on that tractor! Get on the field and do something!'"

Mark Henderson, an inmate at Norfolk State Prison serving 15 years for burglary, had been granted a one-day leave, and all game long had been driving the tractor that belonged to general manager Bucko Kilroy, clearing the yard lines of snow. As Smith and holder Matt Cavanaugh chipped away at the ice with their cleats, out came Henderson on his tractor. The Miami Dolphins thought nothing of it as Henderson drove down the 20–yard line — he had been a presence for most of the day. But then Henderson veered toward Smith and Cavanaugh and cleared a spot for Smith to kick from.

The kick was good and the Patriots won a 3–0 game. The Dolphins were furious, but the officials allowed the field goal to stand. "It was legal," explained referee Bob Frederic. "The game officials have no control over something like that."

It was a bizarre scene, but nothing football couldn't handle. There have been moments of deeper gravity — Walter Payton's game against New Orleans in 1984 when he broke Jim Brown's career rushing record — and even sillier times in the National Football League. Who can forget Miami placekicker Garo Yepremian's attempted pass in Super Bowl VII?

Here is a collection of 10 such instances, from the sublime to the ridiculous. They are part of the NFL's vast treasury of great moments.

95

FOOTBALL FOR THE MASSES

DECEMBER 6, 1925
CHICAGO 19, NEW YORK GIANTS 7

He had come galloping out of the University of Illinois as a three time All-America halfback in 1925, straight into the NFL. And it literally was a game saving run for Harold "Red" Grange, because he made the professional game matter — for the first time — to the American public. Nowhere was this more evident than in the Bears-Giants contest of December 6, 1925.

In his last college game, the "Galloping Ghost" had rushed for 192 yards, completed a touchdown pass, and intercepted a pass to guarantee Illinois a 14–9 victory over Ohio State. In the locker room after the game, Grange revealed he would sign a contract with the Chicago Bears in which he was to receive $3,000 per game and a percentage of the gate each time he played. Grange

had so transcended the college game that many people — including his own coach, Bob Zuppke — didn't want to see him sullied by the professional game.

"You get paid for coaching, Zup," Grange reasoned. "Why should it be so wrong for me to get paid for playing? I'll play football, because that's what I can do best."

On Thanksgiving Day, 10 days after beating the Buckeyes, Grange took the field for the Bears. Though it was snowing, 36,000 spectators — the most ever to see a NFL game to that point — turned out to see Grange. They were disappointed. The Cardinals' Paddy Driscoll, determined to avoid embarrassment, continually punted the ball away from Grange, who only got his hands on three kicks. His longest return was 20 yards, and he ran only 36 yards on the ground while throwing six incomplete passes. The game ended in a scoreless tie, but Grange took home $12,000 and America's appetite for the professional game had been whetted.

To cash in on Grange's appeal, the Bears put together a barnstorming tour that would include seven games in eleven days. During a game in St. Louis, Grange scored all four touchdowns against a team that included only one professional. Nonetheless, 8,000 fans turned out. In Philadelphia, the number swelled to 35,000 as the Bears beat the Frankford Yellowjackets 14–7. Grange scored both touchdowns and earned $40,000 for his trouble, which he split with agent C.C. ("Cash-and-Carry") Pyle, a theatrical promoter.

When Grange had signed with the Bears, he left Giants' owner Tim Mara bitterly disappointed. Mara wired back to New York that he had lost in a bid for Grange's contract but won an agreement for a later exhibition game. Current Giants' owner Wellington Mara, who was nine years old at the time, remembers the game. "Grange was the top name in football and it was a pretty good game. It didn't provide the quick fix at the gate, but it attracted the attention of the press. It showed that there was potential there."

By the time the traveling show reached New York, 73,000 fans, most of them having bought their tickets in advance, jammed the Polo Grounds to see the player Mara had tried to sign after he bought the franchise for $2,500 in 1925. The Bears won 19–7, with Grange intercepting a pass for a touchdown, and evidence that pro football was ready to come out of the closet was supplied.

A year later, Grange was playing in nearby Yankee Stadium in the newly created American Football League. The enterprise failed and Grange never rose to the heights he had enjoyed at Illinois, though he became a defensive back of some repute. Still, his appearance in New York on December 6, 1925 might have changed the professional game forever.

Red Grange cut a dashing figure on the field and off. His charisma helped popularize professional football at a time when college ball was king.

*The Bears and fullback Bronko
Nagurski ran out to a 10-3 lead over the
Giants in the 1934 championship game,
but Chicago lost its foothold in the
second half. The Giants won, 30-13.*

THE SNEAKERS GAME

DECEMBER 9, 1934
NFL CHAMPIONSHIP GAME
NEW YORK GIANTS 30, CHICAGO 13

His name does not appear on any trophy, but Abe Cohen may have been the most valuable non-player in the New York Giants' championship victory over Chicago in 1934. His role in the "Sneakers Game" has grown into something of a legend over the years.

Even without stars Red Grange and Beattie Feathers in the lineup, the 13–0 Bears were expected to handle the 8–5 Giants that blustery day at the Polo Grounds. Chicago had led the league in rushing, total yards, and scoring. The playing field was covered with ice and the wind out of the northeast was gusting at 20 miles per hour. Giants' captain Ray Flaherty, shivering in the nine degree air, offered a suggestion that would win the game.

"Coach, why not wear basketball shoes?" Flaherty said to coach Steve Owen.

Flaherty had remembered a time at Gonzaga University (located in Spokane, Washington) when his team had beaten the weather under similar circumstances with sneakers. Owen liked the idea, but this being Sunday, the New York sporting goods stores were closed. Cohen, a Giants' fan who oversaw the athletic storeroom at nearby Manhattan College, was immediately dispatched to the campus in search of basketball shoes.

The first half, meanwhile, was a disaster for the Giants. The Bears got a touchdown from Bronko Nagurski, and a Jack Manders field goal made it 10–3 over the Giants, who managed only a Ken Strong field goal. At halftime, the Giants found Cohen and 19 pairs of sneakers waiting for them in the locker room. Nine Giants managed to find a pair that fit.

"Look," said Chicago's Walt Kiesling, as the Giants ran out for the second half, "they're wearing sneakers."

"Good," growled coach George Halas, "step on their toes."

The lead grew to 13–3 after another Manders field goal, but the Giants were finally growing accustomed to their new shoes. With 35,059 cheering in the stands, the Giants scored four touchdowns in the fourth quarter. Ed Danowski threw a 28–yard touchdown pass to Ike Frankian to cut the lead to 13–10, and then three plays later Strong ran 42 yards for another score and a 17–13 lead. Both Danowski and Strong scored again and the Giants had routed the Bears, 30–13.

The Bears had won 18 consecutive games to that point, including the 1933 NFL championship over the Giants, 23–21. This time, however, the shoe was on the other foot.

"That was one of my best teams," Halas said in later years. "We would have repeated as champions if we had done one thing: if we had worn sneakers."

A BARRIER FALLS

There had been black men in professional football before Kenny Washington — 17 to be exact. But when Washington signed a contract with the Los Angeles Rams in 1946, he became the first black athlete to join a *major league* professional team in the history of modern-day sports. Jackie Robinson didn't join baseball's Brooklyn Dodgers until 1947.

Oddly enough, the men that broke the racial barriers in football and baseball shared another common experience: they played in the same backfield at UCLA in 1939.

"Kenny Washington was the greatest football player I have ever seen," Robinson wrote in his last years. "He had everything needed for greatness — size, speed, and tremendous strength.

"I'm sure that he had a deep hurt over the fact that he never had become a national figure in professional sports. It would be a shame if he were to be forgotten."

Washington was UCLA's best tailback ever in the three years he served the school, from 1937–39. He established university records in rushing (1,915 yards) and passing (1,300 yards). In his senior season, Washington out–hit Robinson, a transfer from Pasadena City College, by some 200 points in baseball. Those collegiate accomplishments might have been the extent of his sporting success if Cleveland Rams' owner Dan Reeves hadn't been forced to look at Washington in a tryout.

Reeves was moving his team to the West Coast and he desperately wanted the Los Angeles Coliseum as his home field. For 12 years, the NFL owners had an unwritten agreement not to sign black players, but one of the stipulations of the Coliseum management was a tryout for Washington. The league wasn't happy about it, but Reeves signed Washington anyway.

"Reeves had the league over a barrel," Washington said. "The Coliseum people warned the Rams that if they practiced discrimination, they couldn't use the stadium. When those NFL people began thinking about all those seats and the money they could make filling them up, they decided my kind wasn't so bad after all."

Washington was already 28 years old when he joined the Rams and the league's players didn't treat him kindly. His two bad knees were often hit after the referee's whistle blew. Even the addition of former UCLA teammate Woody Strode, a black end, did little to ease the difficulty of Washington's situation. Two years later, after gaining 859 yards, Washington's knees forced him to retire.

By then, Robinson had broken new ground with the Dodgers. Branch Rickey, the Dodgers' owner who signed Robinson, may have been influenced by Washington's success. It could also have been Rickey's experience on the Shelby (Ohio) Athletic Club that influenced his decision to sign Robinson. One of Rickey's teammates on that semi-pro team in 1902 was Charles Follis, a black halfback. Follis, in fact, was the first black man to ever receive money for playing football.

Nonetheless, in 1933 the NFL stopped signing black players. It would take 13 years before Kenny Washington's contract ended that shameful chapter in professional football history.

A year before Jackie Robinson broke the color line in baseball, Kenny Washington was playing for the Los Angeles Rams.

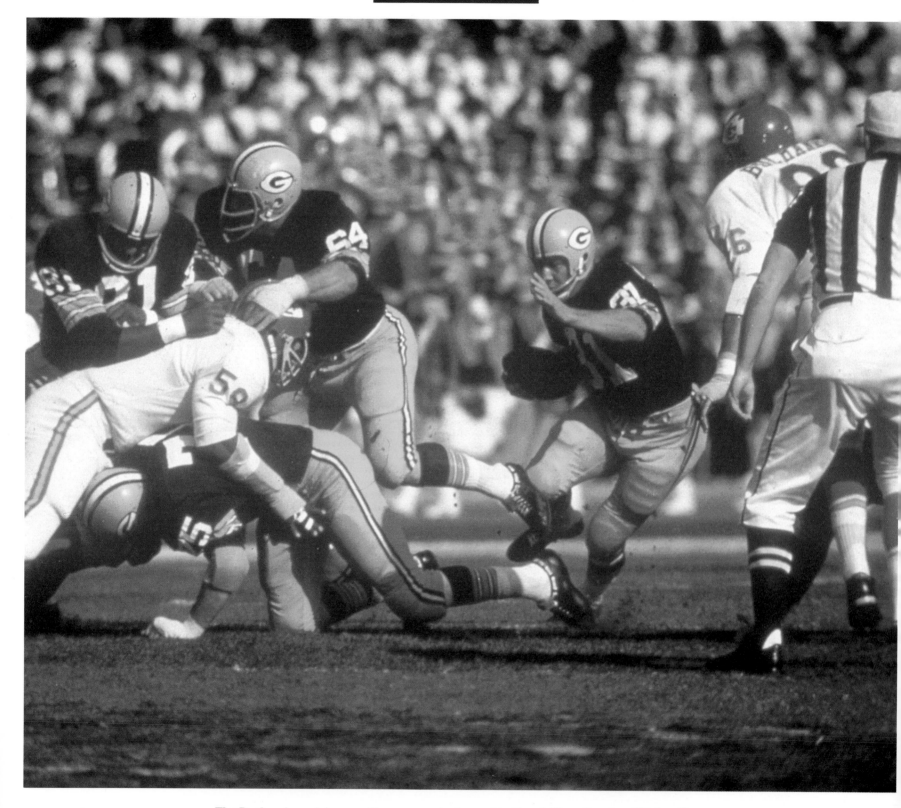

The Packers' precision on offense was a testament to Coach Vince Lombardi's detail.

VINCE LOMBARDI AND A NEW ERA

JANUARY 15, 1967

SUPER BOWL I

GREEN BAY 35, KANSAS CITY 10

There were only 61,946 spectators on hand at Memorial Coliseum in Los Angeles in 1967 for the first edition of what would become America's ultimate sports extravaganza, and some 20,000 seats went begging. Players for the Green Bay Packers received $15,000 each for winning, the largest single game share in the history of team sports at the time but merely pocket change for today's athletes. Though technically it wasn't much to look at, Super Bowl I began a new era for professional football as the Packers beat the Kansas City Chiefs, 35–10.

Vince Lombardi's NFL champions dominated on both sides of the ball, leaving the AFL titlists for dead. Quarterback Bart Starr, along with aging wide receiver Max McGee, made the difference against the Chiefs. Starr, a 17th round draft pick from Alabama in 1956, wasn't the most talented quarterback in the NFL, but he was a proven leader and made the most of his ability.

At the age of 34, McGee had already conceded that Super Bowl I would be his last game. He had caught only three passes all season long playing behind Boyd Dowler, but when Dowler injured his shoulder on the third play of the game, McGee entered the game. Not long afterward, McGee ran a slant-in pattern from the left side. It was third-and–3 and McGee's fake to the outside threw Chiefs cornerback Willie Mitchell off balance. McGee reached back for Starr's underthrown pass at the Kansas City 19 and reeled it in with one hand as Mitchell's dive to break up the pass fell short. McGee pressed the ball against his hip and ran untouched into the end zone for the first touchdown in Super Bowl history.

"When the ball stuck [in my hand] I almost fainted," McGee said. "I expected to open my left hand and find a silver dollar."

Kansas City then tied the score on a 17–yard pass from Len Dawson to Curtis McClinton. On Green Bay's next possession, Starr completed passes for first downs on four consecutive third down plays. The last of those throws set up Jim Taylor's 14–yard sweep around left end. The Packers were leading 21–10 when Starr and McGee connected for another touchdown. On first-and–10 at the Kansas City 13, McGee ran a slant pattern from the left side into the end zone. McGee leaped for the ball, bobbled it, ran under it, and made the catch with studied nonchalance.

McGee finished the game with seven catches for 138 yards and Starr was named the Most Valuable Player for completing 16 of 23 passes for 250 yards. Halfback Elijah Pitts (two touchdowns) and safety Willie Wood, who added an important interception, contributed to the victory. The Packers would win Super Bowl II in similar fashion over the Oakland Raiders with Starr again earning MVP honors.

Yet the rivalry between the leagues had been established. In the next 19 Super Bowls, teams affiliated with the American Football League or Conference would win 12 times.

TOM DEMPSEY'S *63 YARD* FIELD GOAL

NOVEMBER 8, 1970
NEW ORLEANS 19, DETROIT 17

Detroit's Errol Mann kicked the ball up and through the goalposts — good! — and the New Orleans crowd of 66,910 could be forgiven if it exhibited a conditioned response: a collective sigh in the face of yet another loss by their lovable but terrible New Orleans Saints. Mann's 18–yard field goal gave the Lions a 17–16 lead with 14 seconds left in the game and many fans headed for the exits. They would see the Saints lose 40 times in their first

four years of existence — surely, this was just another defeat, albeit coming later than usual in the game.

Those left in the stands didn't take any special notice when Al Dodd returned the Lions' kickoff to the New Orleans 28–yard line. When quarterback Billy Kilmer completed a 17–yard pass to Dodd, the wide receiver skipped out of bounds at the Saints 45–yard line. There were two seconds left and coach J.D. Roberts, coaching his first game for New Orleans after replacing Tom Fears, sent in the field goal unit. The crowd groaned.

"I had no second thoughts," Roberts said, "I knew what Tom Dempsey was capable of."

The placekicker was capable of sending the ball just about anywhere. A year earlier, Dempsey had kicked a 55–yard field goal against the Los Angeles Rams, falling only one yard short of Bert Rechichar's 16–year-old NFL record. On the other hand, Dempsey's length off the tee sometimes translated into erratic shanks and hooks.

Yet, Dempsey was confident; he always had been. Though born without a right hand or right foot, Dempsey had already scored more than 700 points in the NFL. He had already booted three field goals of 27, 28, and 29 yards in this game and a fourth attempt had been blocked by the Lions. Still, this would be a 62–yard attempt — make that 63 yards.

"I set up a little deeper than usual," said holder Joe Scarpati. "I wanted to give Tom time to put something into it. I asked the guys up front to hold [their blocks] a little longer than usual."

The snap came to Scarpati eight yards behind the line of scrimmage from center Jackie Burkett and Dempsey cranked his special square-toed shoe into the football. It seemed straight enough, but would it go far enough? Roberts never saw it flutter over the crossbar — jubilant players obscured his view. The Saints were winners, 19–17, and Dempsey had destroyed Rechichar's record.

"There's so much involved in kicking one that long," Dempsey said after the game, "but I knew I could do it."

Kilmer, sitting in a quiet corner of the locker room, shook his head. "The man just kicked himself into the Hall of Fame, that's all he did today."

And Dempsey's unique shoe is there to this day, a reminder of a record that still stands.

Neither destiny nor the Detroit Lions could deny Tom Dempsey this great moment. His famous field goal traveled 63 yards.

FRANCO HARRIS' "IMMACULATE RECEPTION"

DECEMBER 23, 1972
PITTSBURGH 13, OAKLAND 7

Though it may have been a coincidence, the Pittsburgh Steelers produced their first winning season in nine campaigns the year they drafted a Penn State running back named Franco Harris in the first round. Success came almost instantly to Harris: He was named the 1972 Rookie of the Year and played in the first of nine consecutive Pro Bowls. There would be four Super Bowl victories in the coming years, but never a moment as breathlessly unlikely as the one created by his "Immaculate Reception."

The Steelers blew through the regular season with an 11–3 record and found themselves in their first playoff game in more than a decade. The AFC opponent would be the Oakland Raiders, a team the Steelers beat 34–28 to open the season.

The first half was scoreless. Steelers' kicker Roy Gerela broke the tie in the third quarter with an 18–yard field goal, then added a 29–yarder in the fourth. The Raiders offense had performed dreadfully to that point and coach John Madden benched quarterback Daryle Lamonica in favor of young backup Ken Stabler. With 1:13 left, Stabler turned a broken play into a 30 yard touchdown scramble. The Raiders led, 7–6.

Pittsburgh owner Art Rooney was already in the elevator on his way down to the locker room to console his team when quarterback Terry Bradshaw looked over the Raiders' defense with 22 seconds left on the clock. It was fourth down at the Pittsburgh 40–yard line. Bradshaw took the snap from center and back pedaled into the pocket. Oakland defensive end Tony Cline nearly sacked Bradshaw but somehow he slipped away and spotted running back John "Frenchy" Fuqua downfield. As Bradshaw delivered the ball, Raiders defensive back Jack Tatum threw himself at Fuqua. Tatum and the ball seemed to arrive simultaneously at the Oakland 35–yard line. The result was a weirdly deflected pass that bounced off Tatum's shoulder.

"I was dazed," Fuqua reported later, "then I heard people cheering and I couldn't imagine what happened. So I got up and saw this dude at the 5–yard line and I couldn't figure out why."

Harris, of course, had caught the ball.

"No, I wasn't supposed to be there," Harris said. "In football, you're taught to go to the football and when Terry put it in the air, I took off. I figured Frenchy might need a block if he caught the ball."

As it happened, Harris was directly behind Fuqua when Tatum delivered his crunching blow. Harris gathered the ball in and romped down the left sideline, scoring the winning touchdown with six seconds remaining. The 50,327 Pittsburgh spectators were delirious and the Raiders were furious.

The NFL rule at that time left the touchdown in doubt. In 1972, it wasn't legal for an offensive player to catch a pass after a team-mate had tipped the ball. The officials on the field called the press box to verify the play: Had Tatum touched the ball, or did it pass directly from Fuqua to Harris? The league observer that day was Jim Kensil, who would later become president of the New York Jets. He watched the replay on television and allowed the play to stand. Although Kensil denies it, some observers insist that it was the very first use of instant replay in the NFL.

And so the Steelers won 13–7. They became the Miami Dolphins' 16th consecutive victim a week later, losing the AFC championship game 21–17. Still, the "Immaculate Reception" engineered by Bradshaw and Harris started something special. The Steelers would win four Super Bowl titles in the next seven years.

Harris was moved by his own play. "I guess you could say it was a little bit of luck and God was with us and everything like that," he said. "When you have a feeling that this could be the last play of the season, and that you could blow it, and then one last chance pulls it through for you. . . well, it's beautiful."

The Oakland Raiders' Jack Tatum has already made the big hit on Pittsburgh Steelers' running back Frenchy Fuqua when the ball went on its weird way — into the hands of an amazed Franco Harris.

Garo Yepremian was one of the games most solid kickers. Passing, however, was not his strong suit — especially with millions watching in Super Bowl VII.

GARO PASSES

JANUARY 14, 1973

SUPER BOWL VII

MIAMI 14, WASHINGTON 7

It was folly of the highest (lowest?) magnitude. Garo Yepremian's celebrated attempt to pass the football after his field goal had been blocked in Super Bowl VII has obscured over time the unprecedented achievement of his Miami Dolphins. Yes, Washington Redskins' cornerback Mike Bass won the battle, snatching Yepremian's weak effort and running 49 yards for a touchdown, but the Dolphins won the war, 14–7, finishing the season a perfect 17–0, the best single season record in football history.

Oddly enough, the Dolphins had entered the game against the Washington Redskins at Los Angeles Memorial Coliseum as three point underdogs. Miami had ripped through the regular season, surviving close games against Buffalo and Minnesota. They had defeated the New England Patriots, a team that beat Washington 24–23 that year, by the ridiculous score of 52–0. The Redskins, an 11–3 team over the regular season, beat Green Bay and Dallas by a combined score of 42–6 in the playoffs.

Miami coach Don Shula elected to start Bob Griese over Earl Morrall at quarterback. Griese had fractured an ankle early in the season but had pulled out a 21–17 playoff victory over Pittsburgh to reach the Super Bowl. Before the end of the first quarter, Griese had the Dolphins in the end zone. His 28–yard scoring pass to Howard Twilley on third–and–4 caught the Redskins in man-to-man coverage. Twilley faked cornerback Pat Fischer into a 180–degree turn at the 5-yard-line and Miami led, 7–0.

It became 14–0 in the second quarter when Jim Kiick scored from the 1–yard line. It stayed there for most of the second half.

There were just under two minutes left in the game when Yepremian lined up a 42–yard field goal that would put the game away. Most Valuable Player Jake Scott's 55–yard interception return had given the Dolphins great field position and the running game moved the ball into position for Yepremian. Howard Kindig's snap was low to holder Morrall, but Yepremian hit the ball well. So did Washington tackle Bill Brundige.

The ball fell to the ground and Yepremian picked it up, unaware that he was about to produce one of the memorable moments in football history. Yepremian, inexplicably, tried to throw the ball. Bass, a teammate of Yepremian's when the two played in Detroit, picked the ball out of the air (officially, it was ruled a fumble) and ran 49 yards for a touchdown.

"I thought I saw some white jerseys downfield," Yepremian said later, "that's why I decided to throw the ball. But it just slipped out of my fingers. I thought I was doing something good, something to help the team. Instead, it was almost a tragedy.

Bass recounts the moment this way: "I saw Garo with the ball and I knew from our years in Detroit that he wasn't going to run with it. When it slipped from his hand, he kind of batted it into the air — that's when I got it. I knew Garo wasn't going to tackle me. I'd never let that happen to me or I'd never hear the end of it back in Detroit."

And so it was now 14–7. With 1:57 left on the clock and all their time outs remaining, the Redskins elected to kick deep. Miami ran a minute off the clock and when Bill Stanfill sacked Washington quarterback Billy Kilmer on fourth down the Dolphins — and Yepremian — emerged unscathed.

And Griese was left to shake his head. "I've got to work with Garo," he said, "his throwing technique isn't what it should be."

THE JUICE TOPPLES
A RECORD

DECEMBER 16, 1973
BUFFALO 34, NEW YORK JETS 14

No asterisks are placed beside the records set by players in this era of 16 game seasons, yet maybe there should be. Since 1978, when two games were added to the 14 game schedule, many of football's celebrated marks have been broken in what amounts to a tribute to inflation. This is in no way a slight to the talents of the Los Angeles Rams' Eric Dickerson and Walter Payton of the Chicago Bears, but there was a time when players were measured against more similar criteria.

O.J. Simpson was the bright light of the 1973 season when he made a spectacular run at Jim Brown's single season rushing record of 1,863 yards, set in 1963. "The Juice" was unleashed by an offensive line that called itself the "Electric Company." The results were often breathtaking. He opened the year with a 250-yard effort against the New England Patriots. When Simpson saw the Patriots again in the season's penultimate game, he burned them for 219 yards. That pushed his season's total to 1,803 yards. Only 61 yards separated Simpson from Brown's record.

The last day of the season dawned cold and white; Shea Stadium, where the Bills would meet the New York Jets, was blanketed in snow. Would Simpson be able to keep his feet?

Simpson quickly laid the question to rest as he rushed for 57 yards in Buffalo's opening drive. On the Bills' second possession, Simpson crashed through a hole made by left guard Reggie McKenzie and fullback Jim Braxton. It was a six-yard gain and broke the record.

"Was the hole big enough?" Braxton asked Simpson.

"Looked okay to me," Simpson said. "Let's get some more."

The last of Simpson's 34 carries that day was a seven-yard run behind McKenzie. There was 5:56 left on the clock and the stadium lights had just been turned on, though Simpson hardly needed a spotlight. He finished the day with exactly 200 yards and 2,003 for the season, on 332 carries.

Under the circumstances, his effort was remarkable. Though Brown had carried 41 fewer times in 1963, his blockers were by all accounts superior to Simpson's. And while Brown played for a good team that had many weapons, Simpson was the only serious threat on a team that enjoyed only three winning seasons in his nine years there.

In 1984, Dickerson broke Simpson's record in the 15th game of the season. His final total of 2,105 yards came on 379 carries, an average of 5.5 yards per carry, or approximately a half yard less than Simpson averaged in 1973.

After he broke Brown's record, Simpson revealed that he had seen it coming. "When I was 13 or 14 I once ran into Jimmy Brown in a candy store," Simpson said. "I told him I was going to break his record, like a kid will do. Now that I've done it, it's a little hard to believe."

See New York quarterback Joe Pisarcik reach for the ball. See Philadelphia defensive back Herman Edwards prepare to scoop it up for the winning touchdown. Remember that from this fumble, the Giants gathered themselves for a superb effort in 1986.

THE FUMBLE

NOVEMBER 19, 1978
PHILADELPHIA 19, NEW YORK
GIANTS 17

It wasn't just any fumble. It was a hopelessly bad bounce during the middle of yet another uninspired season, and it served as a metaphor for the frustrations of the Giants and their fans. In a strange and wonderful way, it was the catalyst that set in motion an effort that would culminate in the Giants' long-awaited Super Bowl XXI victory over the Denver Broncos.

The Giants had last appeared in the NFL championship game in three consecutive contests from 1961–63. They lost all three. New York then weathered a series of losing seasons that left fans aching for the glory days of Gifford, Huff, and Robustelli. In 1978, they were coming off five consecutive losing seasons, during which time their combined record was 17–52–1. New York actually opened the season with a modest 5–3 record only to lose three straight games, the last a difficult overtime loss at Washington.

Yet, with 59 1/2 minutes of their game with the Philadelphia Eagles gone, the Giants led 17–12 and seemed on the verge of evening their record and thus suggesting hope for a year of mediocrity. But Giant assistant coach Bob Gibson had other ideas.

While most people expected quarterback Joe Pisarcik to fall on the ball, Gibson called a Pro-Up–65 play from his vantage point in the press box. The players in the huddle grumbled but they had overruled plays so often that season they were afraid to push their luck. Pisarcik took the snap, spun to his left, and dutifully attempted to hand the ball off to fullback Larry Csonka. It glanced off his hip.

Herman Edwards, the Eagles' alert cornerback, scooped up the ball on one bounce and ran it — admittedly in a state of bewilderment — into the end zone for a 26–yard touchdown. Philadelphia won the game, 19–17, and a lot of Giants lost their heads.

Gibson was fired the next day. General Manager Andy Robustelli retired to his Stamford, Connecticut travel agency, and George Young was hired in his place. Coach John McVay was asked to leave and eventually surfaced as the general manager of the San Francisco 49ers. Young hired Ray Perkins to replace him. Together, Young and Perkins used their first round pick to draft a raw quarterback from Moorehead State. Soon Phil Simms was playing ahead of Pisarcik, who left the team a year later.

Perkins would be lured to Alabama in 1982, but the nucleus he and Young built finally arrived during the 1986 season. The Giants won their last 12 games of the season and destroyed the Broncos 39–20 in Super Bowl XXI. Simms, who completed 22 of 25 passes, was the Most Valuable Player.

"There," said Simms after all the ghosts had been laid to rest, "we finally did it. Now, I don't want to hear any more questions about The Fumble."

The Walter Payton legend was certified on October 7, 1984, against the New Orleans Saints. A Toss-28-Weak play turned into a six-yard gain and Payton was the NFL's all-time leading rusher.

SWEETNESS BREAKS THE ALL-TIME RUSHING RECORD

OCTOBER 7, 1984
CHICAGO 20, NEW ORLEANS 7

Men have been running with the football for the better part of a century, but no one has officially run farther in the NFL than Walter Payton of the Chicago Bears. For sheer grace and utter determination, "Sweetness" is unmatched.

Through the 1986 season, Payton had carried the ball 3,692 times for 16,193 yards — more than nine miles through the minefields of the NFL. Both figures are far and away NFL records. Cleveland's Jim Brown, the legend against which Payton is often measured, is second with 12,312 yards.

As the season opened in 1984, that was the all-time mark Payton was aiming for. The 5–foot–10, 202–pound halfback had enjoyed a modest rookie year in 1975, gaining 679 yards, and then producing five consecutive NFC rushing titles and six straight 1,000–yard seasons. The strike of 1982 ended that streak, but Payton's numbers didn't wane. He gained 1,421 yards in 1983 to close in on Brown.

Though Payton turned 30 during training camp, he didn't look his age once the season began. Sixteen carries in the opener against Tampa Bay netted 61 yards. The Denver Broncos watched in amazement the next week as Payton carried 20 times for 179 yards — including a 72–yard jaunt. With the nation's eyes on his every step, Payton put together three more 100–yard games — Green Bay yielded 110, Seattle's contribution was 116 yards, and Dallas' was 155. He was now only 52 yards behind Brown.

On October 10, the New Orleans Saints visited Chicago's Soldier Field. After starting the season 3–0, the Bears had stumbled, losing badly to the Seahawks and then the Cowboys. The Saints represented a chance for redemption, but the Bears fans had come only to see Payton. They weren't disappointed.

Payton gained 50 yards in the first half, falling only two yards short of Brown's career record. On the second play of the third quarter, wide receiver Dennis McKinnon ran in motion from right to left and Jim McMahon took the snap from center Jay Hilgenberg. The play called was a Toss–28–Weak. Fullback Matt Suhey and left guard Mark Bortz hit the New Orleans line, leaving a small crease for Payton. He turned it into a six-yard gain and one of football's most cherished records was his. Payton finished with 154 yards.

"I'm glad I don't have to do this every week," Payton said afterward. "Maybe when the season's over and we win the Super Bowl we can all sit around and reminisce."

Though the Bears wouldn't win the Super Bowl until the end of the 1985 season, Payton's performance would leave a lot of people reminiscing about Brown and another great Chicago running back, Gale Sayers.

After Payton had made his historical run and bounced back into the Bears huddle, Hilgenberg looked across the line of scrimmage. "All right you guys," Hilgenberg said, addressing the Saints, "don't tackle him for a loss on the next play and make us go through all of this again."

1869 • Rutgers defeats Princeton, 6–4, in a soccer-rugby affair that is considered the first football game ever played.

1892 • The Allegheny Athletic Association of Pennsylvania makes William Heffelfinger, an All-America guard from Yale, the first professional player in history. Heffelfinger takes home $500 for an appearance against the Pittsburgh Athletic Club.

1904 • A field goal is changed from five points to four.

1921 • A Chicago Staleys end named George Halas leads the APFA with three touchdown receptions.

1925 • Tim Mara buys the New York Giants franchise for $500.

1927 • The head slap is outlawed.

1939 • NFL regular-season attendance passes 1 million for the first time in history.

1943 • Sammy Baugh of the Washington Redskins leads the NFL in passing, punting, and interceptions.

1947 • Pete Rozelle is hired as public relations man for the Los Angeles Rams by assistant general manager Tex Schramm.

1951 • Despite fielding a team that played for the NFL title, the Rams stop televising home games, citing the loss of $300,000 in gate receipts.

1952 • The Pittsburgh Steelers become the last team to abandon the Single-wing in favor of the T-formation.

1956 • Grabbing the face mask of an opponent (except the ball carrier's) becomes illegal.

1906 • The forward pass is legalized.

1909 • A field goal is changed from four points to the present-day three.

1920 • Jim Thorpe, the player-coach of the Canton Bulldogs, is named President of the American Professional Football Association, the forerunner of the National Football League.

1929 • A field judge is added to the officials unit, raising the number to four.

1931 • Alabama end Don Hutson and quarterback Dixie Howell create the first predetermined pass routes.

1936 • The NFL holds its first college draft.

1940 • Red Barber makes the first radio call of an NFL championship game. A network of 120 stations carries the 73–0 Chicago Bears' victory over the Washington Redskins.

1940 • Byron R. "Whizzer" White leads the NFL with 514 yards rushing for the Detroit Lions. Twenty-two years later, White is named to the Supreme Court.

1943 • All NFL players are required to wear helmets for the first time.

1948 • Los Angeles Rams halfback Fred Gehrke paints horns on his headgear, thereby creating the first emblem on a modern football helmet.

1949 • The Chicago Bears draft an obscure quarterback from the University of Kentucky in the twelfth round. George Blanda finishes his career 26 seasons later with 4,007 passing attempts and 335 field goals.

1950 • The Los Angeles Rams become the first team to televise all their games, both home and away.

1960 • Chuck Bednarik plays linebacker and center for the Philadelphia Eagles in the NFL championship game. He is the last player to line up on both sides of the ball.

1960 • On the twenty-third ballot, Pete Rozelle is elected NFL Commissioner.

1960 • Lamar Hunt founds the fourth version of the American Football League.

1961 • Canton, Ohio is chosen as the future site of the Pro Football Hall of Fame.

1963 • The New York Titans of the AFL change their name to Jets. The move works; a 5–9 record improves to 5–8–1.

1963 • Commissioner Pete Rozelle suspends Green Bay halfback Paul Hornung and Detroit defensive tackle Alex Karras indefinitely for gambling. They are reinstated a year later.

1966 • NBC and CBS pay $9.5 million for the rights to the first four Super Bowls.

1968 • The New York Jets are leading the Oakland Raiders 32–29 with 1:05 left in the game when NBC cuts away to Heidi, a special children's movie. Most viewers didn't find out until a day later that the Raiders won 43–32 with two late touchdowns.

1972 • The Miami Dolphins become the first team in NFL history to finish a full season with a perfect record: 17–0.

1973 • Miami placekicker Garo Yepremian's 42-yard field goal is blocked in Super Bowl VII and he proceeds to throw the world's most famous non-pass. Nonetheless, the Dolphins escape with a 14–7 victory over Washington.

1979 • Before Super Bowl XIII, Dallas Cowboys linebacker Hollywood Henderson says of Pittsburgh Steelers quarterback Terry Bradshaw, "He couldn't spell 'cat' if you spotted him the 'c' and the 'a.'" The Steelers win 35–31, as

Bradshaw throws four touchdown passes and is named the game's Most Valuable Player.

1982 • The Raiders move to Los Angeles and later win an anti-trust suit against the league that brings millions to owner Al Davis.

1986 • The NFL approves the use of instant replay for its games.

1986 • Philadelphia second-year quarterback Randall Cunningham weathers 72 quarterback sacks, a new NFL record.

1963 • Jim Brown of the Cleveland Browns carries 291 times and gains 1,863 yards, an incredible average of 6.4 yards per carry.

1964 • Pete Gogolak of Cornell signs a contract with Buffalo, making him the NFL's first soccer-style placekicker.

1969 • At poolside, New York Jets quarterback Joe Namath predicts his team, a 17-point underdog, will beat the Baltimore Colts in Super Bowl III. The Jets eventually win, 16–7, in one of the biggest upsets of all time.

1969 • Artificial turf is introduced to football, debuting at the Houston Astrodome. The Oilers lose 14–11, to the Dallas Cowboys.

1974 • Joe Namath models pantyhose on a national television commercial.

1979 • The television ratings war heats up: on the same day that ABC airs Super Bowl XIII (featuring the Pittsburgh Steelers and Dallas Cowboys) CBS televises Black Sunday, a terrorist film about a plan to bomb the Super Bowl during a contest between—you guessed it—

the Steelers and Cowboys. Explosives experts search the stadium before the real contest. Art does not imitate life; no bombs are found.

1981 • The Oakland Raiders become the first team to win the Super Bowl after gaining the playoffs as a wild-card entry. Oakland beats the Philadelphia Eagles, 27–10.

1981 • A CBS-New York Times poll indicates that 48 percent of sports fans prefer football, compared to second-place baseball, at 31 percent.

1986 • One hundred and twenty-seven million fans watch the Chicago Bears' 46–10 Super Bowl XXI victory over the New England Patriots, eclipsing the final episode of M*A*S*H as the most-watched television show in history. Two months later, an estimated 300 million watch the taped delay in China.

1987 • A 24-day players' strike rocks the NFL. Owners field replacement teams for three weeks; fans rebel and stay away from the games in droves. Afterwards, Commissoner Rozelle says he was opposed to the idea of replacements anyway.

ALL-TIME FOOTBALL RECORDS

LEADING LIFETIME RECEIVERS

Player	Years	No.	Yards	Avg.	Long	TD
Charlie Joiner	18	750	12,146	16.2	87	65
Steve Largent	11	694	11,129	16.0	74	87
Charley Taylor	13	649	9,110	14.0	88	79
Don Maynard	15	633	11,834	18.7	87	88
Raymond Berry	13	631	9,275	14.7	70	68
Harold Carmichael	14	590	8,985	15.2	85	79
Fred Biletnikoff	14	589	8,974	15.2	82	76
Harold Jackson	16	579	10,372	17.9	79	76
Lionel Taylor	10	567	7,195	12.7	80	45
Lance Alworth	11	542	10,266	18.9	85	85

LEADING LIFETIME SCORERS — KICKING

Player	Years	TD	FG	PAT	TP
George Blanda	26	9	335	943	2,002
Jan Stenerud	19	0	373	580	1,699
Jim Turner	16	1	304	521	1,439
Mark Moseley	16	0	300	482	1,382
Jim Bakken	17	0	282	534	1,380
Fred Cox	15	0	282	519	1,365
Lou Groza	17	1	234	641	1,349
Gino Cappelletti	11	42	176	350	1,130
Don Cockroft	13	0	216	432	1,080
Garo Yepremian	14	0	210	444	1,074

LEADING LIFETIME PASSERS
(Minimum 1,500 attempts)

Player	Years	Att.	Comp.	Pct. Comp.	Yards	TD	Rating*
Dan Marino	4	2,050	1,249	60.9	16,177	142	95.2
Joe Montana	8	2,878	1,818	63.2	21,498	141	91.2
Dave Krieg	7	1,822	1,046	57.4	13,677	107	84.1
Roger Staubach	11	2,958	1,685	57.0	22,700	153	83.4
Danny White	11	2,546	1,517	59.6	19,068	142	83.2
Sonny Jurgensen	18	4,262	2,433	57.1	32,224	255	82.6
Len Dawson	19	3,741	2,136	57.1	28,711	239	82.6
Ken Anderson	16	4,475	2,654	59.3	32,838	197	81.9
Dan Fouts	14	5,240	3,091	59.0	40,523	244	80.9
Neil Lomax	6	2,247	1,287	57.3	15,989	92	80.7

*Rating points are based on percentage of completed passes, touchdown passes, interceptions, and average gain per pass attempt.

LEADING LIFETIME SCORERS — TOUCHDOWNS

Player	Years	Rush	Pass Rec.	Returns	Total TD
Jim Brown	9	106	20	0	126
Walter Payton	12	106	14	0	120
John Riggins	14	104	12	0	116
Lenny Moore	12	63	48	2	113
Don Hutson	11	3	99	3	105
Franco Harris	13	91	9	0	100
Jim Taylor	10	83	10	0	93
Bobby Mitchell	11	18	65	8	91
Leroy Kelly	10	74	13	3	90
Charley Taylor	13	11	79	0	90

LEADING LIFETIME RUSHERS

Player	Years	Att.	Yards	Avg.	Long	TD
Walter Payton	12	3,692	16,193	4.4	76	106
Jim Brown	9	2,359	12,312	5.2	80	106
Franco Harris	13	2,949	12,120	4.1	75	91
Tony Dorsett	10	2,625	11,580	4.4	99	71
John Riggins	14	2,916	11,352	3.9	66	104
O.J. Simpson	11	2,404	11,236	4.7	94	61
Earl Campbell	8	2,187	9,407	4.3	81	74
Jim Taylor	10	1,941	8,597	4.4	84	83
Joe Perry	14	1,737	8,378	4.8	78	53
Larry Csonka	11	1,891	8,081	4.3	54	64

LEADING LIFETIME KICKOFF RETURNERS
(Minimum 75 returns)

Player	Years	No.	Yards	Avg.	Long	TD
Gale Sayers	7	91	2,781	30.6	103	6
Lynn Chandnois	7	92	2,720	29.6	93	3
Abe Woodson	9	193	5,538	28.7	105	5
Claude (Buddy) Young	6	90	2,514	27.9	104	2
Travis Williams	5	102	2,801	27.5	105	6
Joe Arenas	7	139	3,798	27.3	96	1
Clarence Davis	8	79	2,140	27.1	76	0
Lenny Lyles	12	81	2,161	26.7	103	3
Steve Van Buren	8	76	2,030	26.7	98	3
Mercury Morris	8	111	2,947	26.5	105	3

LEADING LIFETIME INTERCEPTORS

Player	Years	No.	Yards	Avg.	Long	TD
Paul Krause	16	81	1,185	14.6	81	3
Emlen Tunnell	14	79	1,282	16.2	55	4
Dick (Night Train) Lane	14	68	1,207	17.8	80	5
Ken Riley	15	65	596	9.2	66	5
Dick LeBeau	13	62	762	12.3	70	3
Emmitt Thomas	13	58	937	16.2	73	5
Bobby Boyd	9	57	994	17.4	74	4
Johnny Robinson	12	57	741	13.0	57	1
Mel Blount	14	57	736	12.9	52	2
Lem Barney	11	56	1,077	19.2	71	7
Pat Fischer	17	56	941	16.8	69	4

PRO FOOTBALL HALL OF FAME

The Professional Football Hall of Fame was founded in Canton, Ohio, in 1963. Members are elected annually by a 29-member board consisting of media representatives from each league city and the president of the Professional Football Writers of America. Each nominee must receive at least 80% of the votes to be elected; four to seven members are elected each year.

Herb Adderley	Daniel Fortmann	Dante Lavelli	Pete Pihos
Lance Alworth	Frank Gatski	Bobby Layne	Hugh (Shorty) Ray
Doug Atkins	Bill George	Tuffy Leemans	Dan Reeves
Morris (Red) Badgro	Frank Gifford	Bob Lilly	Jim Ringo
Cliff Battles	Sid Gillman	Vince Lombardi	Andy Robustelli
Sammy Baugh	Otto Graham	Sid Luckman	Art Rooney
Chuck Bednarik	Red Grange	Link Lyman	Pete Rozelle
Bert Bell	Joe Greene	Tim Mara	Gale Sayers
Bobby Bell	Forrest Gregg	Gino Marchetti	Joe Schmidt
Raymond Berry	Lou Groza	George Marshall	O.J. Simpson
Charles Bidwell	Joe Guyon	Ollie Matson	Bart Starr
George Blanda	George Halas	Don Maynard	Roger Staubach
Jim Brown	Ed Healey	George McAfee	Ernie Stautner
Paul Brown	Mel Hein	Mike McCormack	Ken Strong
Roosevelt Brown	Pete Henry	Hugh McElhenny	Joe Stydahar
Willie Brown	Arnold Herber	John (Blood) McNally	Fran Tarkenton
Dick Butkus	Bill Hewitt	Mike Michalske	Charlie Taylor
Tony Canadeo	Clarke Hinkle	Wayne Millner	Jim Taylor
Joe Carr	Elroy (Crazy Legs) Hirsch	Bobby Mitchell	Jim Thorpe
Guy Chamberlin	Paul Hornung	Ron Mix	Y.A. Tittle
Jack Christiansen	Ken Houston	Lenny Moore	George Trafton
Dutch Clark	Cal Hubbard	Marion Motley	Charlie Trippi
George Connor	Sam Huff	George Musso	Emlen Tunnell
Jim Conzelman	Lamar Hunt	Bronko Nagurski	Clyde (Bulldog) Turner
Larry Csonka	Don Hutson	Joe Namath	Johnny Unitas
Willie Davis	John Henry Johnson	Greasy Neale	Gene Upshaw
Len Dawson	Deacon Jones	Ernie Nevers	Norm Van Brocklin
Art Donovan	Sonny Jurgensen	Ray Nitschke	Steve Van Buren
Paddy Driscoll	Walt Kiesling	Leo Nomellini	Doak Walker
Bill Dudley	Frank (Bruiser) Kinard	Merlin Olsen	Paul Warfield
Turk Edwards	Curly Lambeau	Jim Otto	Bob Waterfield
Weeb Ewbank	Dick (Night Train) Lane	Steve Owen	Arnie Weinmeister
Tom Fears	Jim Langer	Clarence (Ace) Parker	Bill Willis
Ray Flaherty	Willie Lanier	Jim Parker	Larry Wilson
Len Ford	Yale Lary	Joe Perry	Alex Wojciechowicz

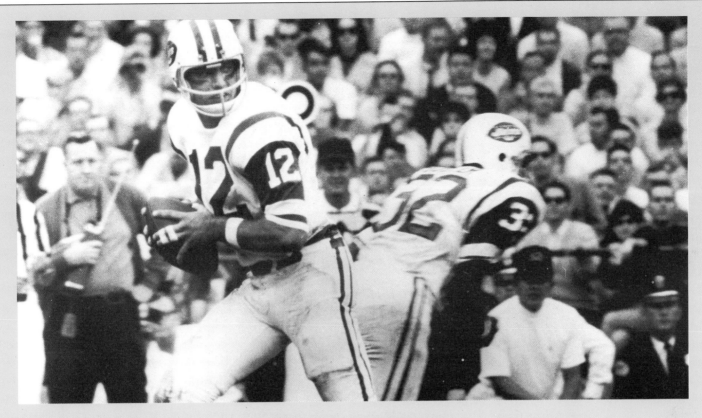

SUPER BOWL RESULTS

Year	Winner	Loser	Site
1967	Green Bay Packers, 35	Kansas City Chiefs, 10	Los Angeles Coliseum
1968	Green Bay Packers, 33	Oakland Raiders, 14	Orange Bowl, Miami
1969	New York Jets, 16	Baltimore Colts, 7	Orange Bowl, Miami
1970	Kansas City Chiefs, 23	Minnesota Vikings, 7	Tulane Stadium, New Orleans
1971	Baltimore Colts, 16	Dallas Cowboys, 13	Orange Bowl, Miami
1972	Dallas Cowboys, 24	Miami Dolphins, 3	Tulane Stadium, New Orleans
1973	Miami Dolphins, 14	Washington Redskins, 7	Los Angeles Coliseum
1974	Miami Dolphins, 24	Minnesota Vikings, 7	Rice Stadium, Houston
1975	Pittsburgh Steelers, 16	Minnesota Vikings, 6	Tulane Stadium, New Orleans
1976	Pittsburgh Steelers, 21	Dallas Cowboys, 17	Orange Bowl, Miami
1977	Oakland Raiders, 32	Minnesota Vikings, 14	Rose Bowl, Pasadena
1978	Dallas Cowboys, 27	Denver Broncos, 10	Superdome, New Orleans
1979	Pittsburgh Steelers, 35	Dallas Cowboys, 31	Orange Bowl, Miami
1980	Pittsburgh Steelers, 31	Los Angeles Rams, 19	Rose Bowl, Pasadena
1981	Oakland Raiders, 27	Philadelphia Eagles, 10	Superdome, New Orleans
1982	San Francisco 49ers, 26	Cincinnati Bengals, 21	Silverdome, Pontiac, Michigan
1983	Washington Redskins, 27	Miami Dolphins, 17	Rose Bowl, Pasadena
1984	Los Angeles Raiders, 38	Washington Redskins, 9	Tampa Stadium
1985	San Francisco 49ers, 38	Miami Dolphins, 16	Stanford Stadium, Palo Alto, California
1986	Chicago Bears, 46	New England Patriots, 10	Superdome, New Orleans
1987	New York Giants, 39	Denver Broncos, 20	Rose Bowl, Pasadena
1988	Washington Redskins, 42	Denver Broncos, 10	Jack Murphy Stadium, San Diego

NUMBER-ONE DRAFT CHOICES

Year	Team	Player	Position	College
1988	Atlanta	Aundray Bruce	LB	Auburn
1987	Tampa Bay	Vinny Testaverde	QB	Miami
1986	Tampa Bay	Bo Jackson	RB	Auburn
1985	Buffalo	Bruce Smith	DE	Virginia Tech
1984	New England	Irving Fryar	WR	Nebraska
1983	Baltimore	John Elway	QB	Stanford
1982	New England	Kenneth Sims	DT	Texas
1981	New Orleans	George Rogers	RB	South Carolina
1980	Detroit	Billy Sims	RB	Oklahoma
1979	Buffalo	Tom Cousineau	LB	Ohio State
1978	Houston	Earl Campbell	RB	Texas
1977	Tampa Bay	Ricky Bell	RB	Southern California
1976	Tampa Bay	Lee Roy Selmon	DE	Oklahoma
1975	Atlanta	Steve Bartkowski	QB	California
1974	Dallas	Ed Jones	DE	Tennessee State
1973	Houston	John Matuszak	DE	Tampa
1972	Buffalo	Walt Patulski	DE	Notre Dame
1971	New England	Jim Plunkett	QB	Stanford
1970	Pittsburgh	Terry Bradshaw	QB	Louisiana Tech
1969	Buffalo	O.J. Simpson	RB	Southern California
1968	Minnesota	Ron Yary	T	Southern California
1967	Baltimore	Bubba Smith	DT	Michigan State
*1966	Atlanta	Tommy Nobis	LB	Texas
	Miami	Jim Grabowski	FB	Illinois
1965	New York Giants	Tucker Frederickson	HB	Auburn
	Houston	Lawrence Elkins	E	Baylor
1964	San Francisco	Dave Parks	E	Texas Tech
	Boston	Jack Concannon	QB	Boston College
1963	Los Angeles	Terry Baker	QB	Oregon State
	Kansas City	Buck Buchanan	DT	Grambling
1962	Washington	Ernie Davis	HB	Syracuse
	Oakland	Roman Gabriel	QB	North Carolina State
1961	Minnesota	Tommy Mason	HB	Tulane
	Buffalo	Ken Rice	G	Auburn
1960	Los Angeles Rams	Billy Cannon	HB	Louisiana State
1959	Green Bay	Randy Duncan	QB	Iowa
1958	Chicago Cardinals	King Hill	QB	Rice
1957	Green Bay	Paul Hornung	QB	Notre Dame
1956	Pittsburgh	Gary Glick	DB	Colorado A&M
1955	Baltimore	George Shaw	QB	Oregon
1954	Cleveland	Bobby Garrett	QB	Stanford
1953	San Francisco	Harry Babcock	E	Georgia
1952	Los Angeles	Bill Wade	QB	Vanderbilt
1951	New York Giants	Kyle Rote	HB	Southern Methodist
1950	Detroit	Leon Hart	E	Notre Dame
1949	Philadelphia	Chuck Bednarik	C	Pennsylvania
1948	Washington	Harry Gilmer	QB	Alabama
1947	Chicago Bears	Bob Fenimore	HB	Oklahoma A&M

1946	Boston	Frank Dancewicz	QB	Notre Dame
1945	Chicago Cardinals	Charley Trippi	HB	Georgia
1944	Boston	Angelo Bertelli	QB	Notre Dame
1943	Detroit	Frank Sinkwich	HB	Georgia
1942	Pittsburgh	Bill Dudley	HB	Virginia
1941	Chicago Bears	Tom Harmon	HB	Michigan
1940	Chicago Cardinals	George Cafego	HB	Tennessee
1939	Chicago Cardinals	Ki Aldrich	C	Texas Christian
1938	Cleveland	Corbett Davis	FB	Indiana
1937	Philadelphia	Sam Francis	FB	Nebraska
1936	Philadelphia	Jay Berwanger	HB	Chicago

Note: For the period 1961–66, both the NFL and AFL number-one picks are listed.
(The AFL had been formed in 1960 but had no formal first pick that year.) The leagues merged in 1966.

CLUB ADDRESSES

American Football Conference

BUFFALO BILLS
One Bills Drive
Orchard Park, New York 14127
(716) 648-1800

CINCINNATI BENGALS
200 Riverfront Stadium
Cincinnati, Ohio 45202
(513) 621-3550

CLEVELAND BROWNS
Cleveland Stadium
Cleveland, Ohio 44114
(216) 696-5555

DENVER BRONCOS
5700 Logan Street
Denver, Colorado 80216
(303) 296-1982

HOUSTON OILERS
6910 Fannin Street
Houston, Texas 77030
(713) 797-9111

INDIANAPOLIS COLTS
P.O. Box 24100
Indianapolis, IN 46224-0100
(317) 297-2658

KANSAS CITY CHIEFS
One Arrowhead Drive
Kansas City, Missouri 64129
(816) 924-9300

LOS ANGELES RAIDERS
332 Center Street
El Segundo, California 90245
(213) 322-3451

MIAMI DOLPHINS
4770 Biscayne Blvd., Suite 1440
Miami, Florida 33137
(305) 576-1000

NEW ENGLAND PATRIOTS
Sullivan Stadium — Route 1
Foxboro, Massachusetts 02035
(617) 543-8200

NEW YORK JETS
598 Madison Avenue
New York, New York 10022
(212) 421-6600
or practice:
1000 Fulton Avenue
Hempstead, New York 11550
(516) 538-6600

PITTSBURGH STEELERS
Three Rivers Stadium
300 Stadium Circle
Pittsburgh, Pennsylvania 15212
(412) 323-1200

SAN DIEGO CHARGERS
San Diego-Jack Murphy Stadium
9449 Friars Road
San Diego, California 92120
(619) 280-2111

SEATTLE SEAHAWKS
11220 N.E. 53rd Street
Kirkland, Washington 98033
(206) 827-9777

National Football Conference

ATLANTA FALCONS
Suwanee Road at I-85
Suwanee, Georgia 30174
(404) 945-1111

CHICAGO BEARS
Halas Hall,
250 N. Washington Road
Lake Forest, Illinois 60045
(312) 295-6600

DALLAS COWBOYS
Cowboys Center
1 Cowboys Parkway
Irving, TX 75063-4727
(214) 556-9900

DETROIT LIONS
1200 Featherstone Road
Pontiac, Michigan 48057
(313) 335-4131

GREEN BAY PACKERS
1265 Lombardi Avenue
Green Bay, Wisconsin 54303
(414) 494-2351

LOS ANGELES RAMS
2327 W. Lincoln Avenue
Anaheim, California 92801
(714) 535-7267

MINNESOTA VIKINGS
9520 Viking Drive
Eden Prairie, Minnesota 55344
(612) 828-6500

NEW ORLEANS SAINTS
6928 Saints Avenue
Metairie, Louisiana 70003
(504) 733-0255

NEW YORK GIANTS
Giants Stadium
East Rutherford,
New Jersey 07073
(201) 935-8111

PHILADELPHIA EAGLES
Broad Street & Pattison Avenue
Philadelphia, Pennsylvania 19148
(215) 463-2500

ST. LOUIS CARDINALS
Busch Stadium, P.O. Box 888
St. Louis, Missouri 63188
(314) 421-0777

SAN FRANCISCO 49ERS
711 Nevada Street
Redwood City, California 94061
(415) 365-3420

TAMPA BAY BUCCANEERS
One Buccaneer Place
Tampa, Florida 33607
(813) 870-2700

WASHINGTON REDSKINS
P.O. Box 17247
Dulles International Airport
Washington, D.C. 20041
(703) 471-9100

INDEX

PHOTO CREDITS